Heaven's
Greater
Government

Behind the Scenes of Earth's Events

JEANNE METCALF

Cëgullah Publishing
International Copyright © 2022
Cegullah Publishing and Apologetics
Academy
International Copyright © 2024
www.cegullahpublishing.ca

Textbook: ISBN 978-1-926489-44-5
Workbook: ISBN 978-1-926489-43-8

All scripture quotes originate from KJV[1], public domain. However, the name of God appears as YeHoVaH, not LORD. See appendix for more information.

---

[1]KJV refers to all humankind as "man". Unless the passage itself refers to a particular male person, apply the message to all humankind, regardless of gender.

Dedication

If you, dear Reader, wish to receive an understanding of the spiritual reality of Heaven's government and bow to its rulership in your life, then, *to you* I dedicate this book. May the Living and True God transform your entire being wherever necessary so that you may recognize, embrace, honour, and function in the power of Heaven's greater government.

COURSE 201

Section 1
RULING IN THE BEGINNING
(*Before* Day 7)

COURSE 202

Section 2
RULING IN THE EARTH
(*On* Day 7)

Section 3
RULING IN THE HEAVENLIES
(*After* Day 7's Victory)

APPENDIX

[2] A prophetic view

COURSE 201
Heaven's Greater Government

יְהֹוָה

SECTION 1:
RULING IN THE BEGINNING

(*Before* Day 7)

Introduction

"And he (Yeshua) said unto them (His disciples), When ye pray, say, Our Father which art in heaven, Hallowed be thy name. Thy kingdom come. Thy will be done, as in heaven, so in earth."

Luke 11:2

It was spring in the small town of Preston, Ontario, Canada. Rays of sunshine awakened the early flowers and birds, singing their joyous ode to spring, worked hard to build their nests. Shop owners on the main street of the town, with broom in hand, swept the sidewalks, while window washers cleaned the large store front windows. It was a busy time indeed, especially for a small shop owner named Elsie.

Elsie, a woman in her fifties, managed her own store named, Vanity Fair. Elite buyers frequented her store along with those seeking wedding garments, prom dresses and other special seasoned apparel. Vanity Fair, "the" place in town to shop for women's clothing, was extremely busy, but at this point in the spring, not with buyers! No, early in the spring Elsie planned for her yearly spring fashion show. This show, the highlight of the year, enjoyed great attendance, and every year, the top reporter of the town newspaper highlighted the event.

Elsie, along with my mother, Lorraine, worked hard planning for this spring event. Everything went like clockwork, following an established pattern of former, successful fashion shows. First, Elsie phoned the models, ranging in age from 12 to 60. Each model had a time slot to come to the store for a fitting. Next, as each model arrived, Elsie and my mother fitted them with outfits. A trail of clothing consisting of summer swimming apparel, sun dresses, formal and semi formal gowns along with hats, gloves, and shoes, stretched from store showroom to fitting room, day after day for nearly two weeks. At the end of this sorting process, several racks of specially selected outfits stood in a safe place in the store, waiting for the expected day.

With the walk down the runway of the Preston theatre only 4 days away, Elsie, following her yearly routine, phoned her trusted friend who always wrote the script for the show. After the normal cordial greeting, Elsie began to state her business, then stopped midway, rudely interrupted by her friend. Quietly, she put the phone back into its cradle, ending the call. She sat down on a nearby chair. Moments later, she looked at my mother who by this time was right by her side. "Lorraine," said Elsie, "I hate to tell you this, but I have to cancel the fashion show."

Shocked, my mother asked the reason for this sudden decision. Elsie reported that her friend, who always wrote the script for the show, due to health issues, could not do it this year. Elsie had no substitute. Left with no choice, she must cancel the show. My mother, one who never gave up on anything, decided someone else must write the copy and she knew exactly who that person might be. Elsie gave my mother two days to prove to her that her suggested writer could do the job well enough to satisfy her. If not, then Elsie would make that dreaded phone call and cancel the show.

After 6 o'clock pm, when the shop closed, my mother came home. As usual, we sat down at the supper table together as a family. My mother sat at one end of the table, my father at the other end, and we three children, all in our early teen years, sat on the left-hand side of the table arranged by birth order. My brother sat near to my father, my sister near to my mother, and I sat in the middle. Dad spoke about the events of his day;

then my mother debriefed on her day. We listened carefully as mom related how the fashion show came dangerously close to being cancelled, but she had a plan!

Wondering what that plan might be, we continued to eat our meal as mother explained further. Elsie needed a writer to complete her fashion show. No ordinary writer would do either. This writer needed to articulate with clear and precise description what each outfit entailed. Also, the narrative must draw buyers, to purchase, for while the show gave enjoyment to its onlookers, it must produce a profit for Vanity Fair. A good narrative ensured a successful show, while a bad one guaranteed failure.

Mother knew just the person to write for Elsie. With confidence mother boasted that she and her newfound writer would save the show! How exciting I thought, but that excitement quickly disappeared for mother turned to me. "Jeanne", she said, "you received an A+ on your recent essay in your literature class last week. You will write the script for the show." Excuse me! Mother and I would save the fashion show! You have got to be kidding!

Excuses never worked well with my mother. Not to mention the two-day deadline gave no room to prove to mother that I was not the person. No! This situation eliminated any pleas to get out of the job. Before I knew it, I was in a car and on my way to Vanity Fair to see the "objects" of my creative writing assignment. That very evening, with pen and paper in hand I became a fashion writer! Well, at least that is what my imagination told me.

Two-days later, Elsie received the script and reviewed it, immediately. Mom waited for Elsie's review, which came shortly before the store's closing. With the shop closed up, mom headed for home to convey the verdict to waiting ears.

Once she arrived in the house, we all sat down at the supper table. Dad, as usual, related his day, but I must admit, my attention span in that moment focused on my mother's soon coming report. As mom began her story, she related that she handed the script to Elsie for review. Elsie took the script, reviewed it immediately, leaving mom to tend the store. We heard about how many customers she waited on as Elsie reviewed the script in the back room. Then, we heard how Elsie picked up the phone to make a phone call.

We waited with bated breath to hear if Elsie cancelled the fashion show. Mom, looking my way, smiled at me. Elsie, she related, called the theatre to confirm the fashion show would run as normal. Thrilled by the script she received; Elsie happily went about her business scheduling her fashion show. After the show finished, I'd like to tell you that I received accolades for my writing, or that someone other than my mother said thank you.

While I did hear that people appreciated the fresh approach in the description of the clothes as the models walked down the runway, and that sales were at a one time high, no one shouted at the end of the show, "bring out the author". However, I did hear that my mother received a bonus for saving the fashion show. Oh, and apparently, she told Elsie that I would do it again next year, if need be. Elsie, however, set in following her normal routine, declined the offer. My days as a fashion writer ended as quickly as they started.

BEHIND THE SCENES EVENTS

Elsie's fashion show saw many activities operating in the background as she and others worked to make this event successful. Before the show could go on, however, *in Elsie's mind*, it needed narrative. To Elsie, words, properly written and read, either make or break the show. Words, to Elsie, were paramount!

In many ways, Elsie's fashion show and her attitude hold one thing in common with God's kingdom. That commonality lies in the need for words. Words seemed paramount to Elsie and words are paramount in God's kingdom. God spoke the world into being and set a principle in place as to the effectiveness of words. Through our utterance of words His kingdom

14

comes to pass in our lives. Just as words made the difference between Elsie's fashion show being a success or not, so words in our mouth make the difference between the activity and inactivity of God's government and how it affects our life. Yeshua's very words verify that fact.

Mark 11:23

23 For verily I say unto you, That whosoever shall say unto this mountain, Be thou removed, and be thou cast into the sea; and shall not doubt in his heart, but shall believe that those things which he saith shall come to pass; he shall have whatsoever he saith.

Speak to the mountain, Yeshua said. Believe and you shall have what you said. Yeshua further affirmed the importance of the word connection between earth and God's kingdom when He addressed the subject of prayer. Listen to the first 4 words before Yeshua presented one of the best-known prayers in the world, "The Lord's Prayer" [3]..

Luke 11:2 a

When ye pray, say".

Our words, even in expressing our prayers, have power to bring God's kingdom to pass in your life. As

---

[3]Others title this prayer "The Our Father."

we explore this prayer to our Heavenly Father, after taking time to hallow His wonderful name, we discover two sentences with the potential to change lives.

Thy kingdom come. Thy will be done. [4]

Once our mouth opens and we speak Yeshua's two sentences, we decree a powerful event to take place in our life. With seven simple, yet potent words we release a power of God to live a blessed life upon the earth. No greater blessing exists than to live with God's kingdom ruling over us. His kingdom brings righteousness, peace, and joy in the Holy Spirit![5]

Thus, as we declare these two sentences[6], they become a key in our hands to unlock a door to bring Heaven's government into our life. Additionally, as we petition God on behalf of others, we seek His face to see His kingdom come into their lives, as well. Envision, if you will, the furthest extent of God's kingdom touching lives, like a heavenly mantle stretching over the whole earth[7]. What an earth that would be!

THY KINGDOM COME'S IMPACT

Yeshua, in speaking about Heaven, likened it to a kingdom, and often spoke of it. He used phraseology

---

[4] *Matthew 6:10; Luke 11:2*

[5] *Romans 14:17*

[6] "Thy kingdom come. Thy will be done",

[7] This happens in the millennium reign.

16

such as "the kingdom of God" or "the kingdom of Heaven". These two interchangeable terms relate to Heaven's government, which of course, functions within God's kingdom. To understand God's kingdom, our focus shifts from kingdoms we know on earth to foresee one founded and operated by the Sovereign majesty of Heaven and earth. Such a kingdom functions with divine principles, totally *unaffected* by humankind.

As we study Yeshua's words, we see that He invited His disciples for all generations *to speak* the words He commanded and enjoy the response. As His disciples do this, the King of Heaven responds to the words uttered, receiving them as a command. He receives the words as a legal declaration inviting Him to reign over us. In response to that command, God makes His kingdom a reality in the life of those who desire it. Each petitioner, uttering the words, "Thy kingdom come. Thy will be done", as Yeshua taught, can expect the kingdom's arrival and God's will fulfilled.

WHAT WORDS PRODUCE
Thus, Yeshua's disciples, then and through all generations, look *in faith* to the Heavenly Father, to Whom the prayer addresses, to realize in their lives the fullest possible manifestation of His government upon the earth. However, the eyes of faith understand the realization of that governmental rule comes in a slightly different format upon the earth than in heaven.

Nevertheless, as we speak, "Thy kingdom come. "Thy will be done.", we add our personal choice to bow our knees to Heaven's greater government, submitting willingly to the rule of the King. With heart and tongue aligned in submission to the One Who created them, each one who prayed these words prepares to receive God's orders for their life, living it out to honour Him, to the best of their ability.

This is the foundational meaning of
"Thy kingdom come. Thy will be done. "

INFLUENCE OF HEAVEN'S GOVERNMENT
Those truly submitted to God, who desire to see the fullest possible manifestation of His government, know that the present influence of Heaven's government must increase in greater measure, first, in their personal life, if they are to affect the world around them. Nevertheless, in the interim, the heart that *begins* to enjoy the rule of God over their life *grows* into a life yielded to truth and obedience to the Word of God, which in turn helps us to control the words we utter from our mouth. Here, again, words make a difference.

Thus, believers who learn to control their tongue and speak life-giving words, live out their day with the peace and serenity of God, the authority and power of the Majesty on High, and in the Person and presence of God, Himself. Such a one gently walks into their future, within God's present destiny for His kingdom's government upon the earth. These believers expect more to follow. Each believer, as they live the moments, days, and years before them, moves in a closer realm with the Almighty resulting in a satisfying life in God and the manifestation of the government upon the earth as they decree and believe possible.[8] Wow! What power words have as they leave our lips and soar into the invisible world around us!

Additionally, greater depth of God's own Word, its meaning, and its power seeps steadily into the heart of any yielded vessel. Profound truth and wisdom abound in God's world and His words of life bring fulfilment to the ones totally submitted to the living God. Such a heart enjoys great fellowship with God. Such bask in the glorious light of His Being and continues to cry out daily:

"Thy kingdom come. Thy will be done. "

HEAVEN'S GOVERNMENT ACCESSED BY FAITH
Believers knowledgeable in the Word of God understand that the governmental rule of God's kingdom lies hidden behind the scenes, however, prayer, which means the use of the spoken word, accesses the kingdom. Our words, spoken in faith, appropriate what our heart desires to see manifest by

---

[8] *Philippians 3:1-7*

God's power in our world. Unfortunately, people often become discouraged when they pray but don't see an immediate manifestation of God's kingdom.

Reality teaches us that challenges arise when reaching out to see God's government move into our own life as well as the lives of others. Extend faith further and stretch prayers to see a nation's government bow to God's government, and far too often frustrated and disappointed prayer warriors become saddened when they do not see *instant effects* of Heaven's government upon those of the earth. With God's mind and wisdom released into the situation, through the power of the Holy Spirit, one option remains: ***to press into God even further, continuing to trust God and believe their government can and will align with Heaven's government.***

Using the tool of words in prayer, believers expect transformation to come but wisdom dictates leaving the timeframe to God. If the need is immediate, so comes God's response. However, God's overall plans for governments *may* take longer to manifest, depending on God's overall plan for the nation. Keep in mind that an important key to see things happen on the earth lies not by measuring the time required to bring Heaven's government to pass, but rather a focus to remain locked into a faith agreement with God to see things happen, no matter the timeframe.

It always means watching our hearts and words that come out from our mouth so that we do not drift away from words of agreement *spoken earlier* in faith. Keeping our hearts afire with faith, we speak words agreeing with God's plans, seen or unseen, immediate or delayed. On these we focus and not on what our human eyes see. Believers trust in God's sovereignty and ability, putting faith to work.[9] Thus, the believer employs a far greater principle and enters *a rest* to see God's government manifest on the earth.   Prayer warriors and intercessors crying out to God for change, must conclude that, at best, their role forms only part of the whole in the puzzle of prayer activity.

Since the government of God falls into the category of a spiritual reality, the eye of faith opens wide to see and implement such as God directs.   Truly, a spiritual mind, with insight guided by the Holy Spirit, recognizes the greater principles functioning in the government of God, even if only perceived behind the scenes.   They grasp the fact that God longs for kingdom principles to rise to a place of paramount activity on the earth.

Remember Elsie and her fashion show? Recall how she knew that a good script made or broke the fashion

---

[9] *Hebrews 11:6 But without faith it is impossible to please him: for he that cometh to God must believe that he is, and that he is a rewarder of them that diligently seek him.*

show? In Elsie's life, she learned that words made a difference. Likewise, in God's kingdom, words make a difference. Believers who recognize the power of their words effect their life and those of others learn to speak, carefully. A simple utterance of the words of Yeshua, "Thy kingdom come. Thy will be done", act like a mighty script to bring a thing into reality.

Those with a discerning eye see their need for man's will to accept God's will in a greater way and using word power pray to see His principles recognized, received and then, in operation. It may come in small increments, but indeed it will come! Truly, the eye of faith concludes that Heaven's greater government functions upon the earth. Whether we like it or prefer to ignore the thought, the power of words, spoken or left unsaid, make a difference!

God's people who experience doubt have opportunity to refrain from speaking their thoughts and thus, have an open door to learn to speak God-inspired words such as those Yeshua taught His followers to see His kingdom manifest. God, when petitioned helps all to rise above their shortcomings. He enables His people to rise in Holy Spirit empowered faith to see the government of their nation function within the greatest possible capacity on earth … *in alignment with Heaven's government and its principles.* It does come, when our words, prayers and faith align with His will!

HEAVEN'S GOVERNMENT REVEALED

Through this Bible Study[10], dear reader, lies an opportunity to recognize Heaven's government as the scriptures show it operative. Thus, you can receive faith, hope and insight to appropriate the truth, personally. As certain biblical passages under study bring the operation of God's kingdom to life, its visible reality in your life becomes more easily recognized. Living with that truth, you can note Heaven's government operating elsewhere, such as on the world scene. Recognizing God's kingdom active, you can then choose to rest confidently in the One Whose capable power makes it possible for His kingdom to manifest, *in whole or in part, **in any circumstance**.*

UP TO THE CHALLENGE?

Depending on your present theology, learning about the kingdom of God, highlighting that kingdom's operation in all circumstances, may present some challenges. Mindsets, previously formed and firmly established, might stand in the way of helping a person receive *perfect truth*. These mindsets, shaped by numerous former factors, may not align one hundred percent with biblical truth. For example, for centuries people thought that Yeshua of Nazareth, prior to His ministry, made His living as a carpenter.

---

[10] Usually, these studies come with a workbook, which we suggest one does first, before reading the textbook. However, in this case, we recommend reading the textbook first, and then going to the workbook.

Today's findings, using architectural, scriptural, and historical data, point to Yeshua's trade as that of a stone builder. When one considers the lack of wood in Israel compared to the abundance of stone, it seems more logical to assume Yeshua's trade as a stone builder. To accept that, however, one must willingly release a paradigm, a former mindset.

Another paradigm shift comes as we look at the life of Saul (Paul) of Tarsus. For years people thought Paul made tents. However, our Jewish believers say that as a Pharisee, made tallits, Jewish prayer shawls. Apparently, "tallit" in Hebrew means little tent, which refers to the Tabernacle of Moses' day, when every Jew had his own prayer shawl, (or little tent) in which they hid their face to pray. To accept this mindset of Paul's activity, means breaking centuries long traditions of Christianity.

Of course, these truths just related do not shake the foundations of the faith like some which hit harder in centuries past, such as salvation gained by works challenged by the words "the just shall live by faith." That paradigm shift triggered the Great Reformation. Fortunately, today's believer, with access to the original transcripts of the faith, can examine the evidence of scripture and walk in a straighter line with that truth, if they exchange an erroneous paradigm for truth.

A MESSAGE TO THE READER

Dear Reader, as an ardent student of the Word, be encouraged to push through the barrage of human thought to exchange it for divine. Obtain better results by first, becoming aware of the possibility of existing paradigms. When encountering paradigms, resist the anger response. Instead, face the problem, confronting it, immediately. When it comes to understanding scripture, seek God to possess a love for the truth and willingly discard error. Keep an open heart, mind, and ear to the Holy Spirit. Hang in there until the truth of God breaks all erroneous paradigms.

One key to walking above the barrage of problems you might face in walking away from paradigms, rests in remembering this fact: *the Holy Spirit leads into all truth*[11]. Trust Him! Additionally, decide *now* to release all *unbiblical paradigms*, all *erroneous mindsets* previously learned. If that earlier truth does not align one hundred percent with the Word of God, why keep it anyway? Take all considerations about the matter to God in prayer. Allow the Holy Spirit to put things in their proper place as His wisdom dictates.

READY TO GO!

So, dear reader, roll up your sleeves, sharpen your coloured pencils to highlight biblical passages and ready your pen to take notes. Be prepared for your

---

[11] *John 6:1*

25

eyes to open wide with excitement as you travel on this journey extraordinaire. With the Holy Spirit's help, position yourself to take a step forward to discover powerful and effective principles of a far greater government, which operates behind the scenes of earth's events. Get ready, dear reader, move forward, impressed, and even changed as you study and learn to embrace the reality of

Heaven's Greater Government.

CHAPTER'S REFLECTION

"And said, O YeHoVaH God of our fathers, art not thou God in heaven? and rulest not thou over all the kingdoms of the heathen? and in thine hand is there not power and might, so that none is able to withstand thee?"

2 Chronicles 20:6

In The Creator's Plan   1

"Forasmuch as ye know that ye were not redeemed with corruptible things, [as] silver and gold, from your vain conversation [received] by tradition from your fathers; But with the precious blood of Christ, as of a lamb without blemish and without spot: Who verily was foreordained before the foundation of the world, but was manifest in these last times for you," Who by him do believe in God, that raised him up from the dead, and gave him glory; that your faith and hope might be in God."

1 Peter 1:18-21

BUILDINGS which endure over time, rest upon a solid, stable, foundation. This the architect ensures by his wisdom and diligence in the planning stages, as well as his onsite management as the building project takes place. Proper codes, regional requirements, along with quality products, go into the formation of that firm foundation, making the building resting upon it safe for centuries.

If a builder, however, substitutes inferior materials he creates an architectural nightmare. A lack of sound architectural principles, which may well include the removal of the architect's watchful eye, makes the venture, *in whole or in part*, a recipe for disaster. Under such conditions, as the builder produces an inferior foundation, the possibilities of a whole building collapsing increases.

In the end, such a building shifts out of alignment, proving itself unsafe, unusable, and slated for the wrecking ball. However, reverse the situation and apply sound wisdom, and you have a building and foundation which has the potential to endure for centuries.

Most of us, if given a choice which building to purchase and which architect to praise, choose the one built on a firm foundation with an architect we can trust. God, the Master Architect, planned the inception of our universe and its continuance. Resting our universe upon a strong and enduring foundation, He built it to stand the test of time.

Isaiah 48:12-13
   "12 Hearken unto me, O Jacob and Israel, my called; I

am he; I am the first, I also am the last. **13** *Mine hand also hath laid the foundation of the earth, and my right hand hath spanned the heavens: when I call unto them, they stand (endure[12]) up together."*

Here, God calls listeners to sharpen their hearing. Then, He declares an aspect of His all-encompassing being, which stems from "everlasting" to everlasting[13]".

In terms our finite minds grasp, He says:

Isaiah 48:12
**I am He. I am the first (Aleph).
I am also the last (Tov).**

Next, He speaks of the earth's foundation.

Isaiah 48:13
My hand has laid the foundation of the earth & My Right Hand hath spanned the heavens: *when* I call unto them, they stand up together."

Does Scripture name the Right Hand of God, Who laid the foundation of the earth and spanned the heavens? It does. Within the New Testament writings, referring to Yeshua, we hear the answer.

---

[12] Online Bible from Strong's Concordance 05975 עָמַד 'amad awmad' a primitive root meaning to endure, stand the test of time.
[13] *Psalm 90:2*

Colossians 1:16-17

16 For by him (Yeshua) were all things created, that are in heaven, and that are in earth, visible and invisible, whether [they be] thrones, or dominions, or principalities, or powers: all things were created by him, and for him: 17 And he is before all things, and by him all things consist.

Yeshua, the Word[14], Who made all things, stood at the very inception of our universe. It began at His command, and it won't end until He utters that specific command. *In the interim,* He holds it all together by the Word of His Power[15].

EARLY CHURCH VIEWS ON CREATION

These truths regarding Yeshua, the Word of God, the early church knew well.

Revelation 1:17

17 And when I saw him, I fell at his feet as dead. And he laid his right hand upon me, saying unto me, Fear not; I am the first and the last:

John 1:1

1 In the beginning was the Word, and the Word was

---

[14] *"In the beginning was the Word, and the Word was with God, and the Word was God." (John 1:1)*

[15] *"Who being the brightness of [his] glory, and the express image of his person, and upholding all things by the word of his power, when he had by himself purged our sins, sat down on the right hand of the Majesty on high;" (Hebrews 1:3)*

with God, and the Word was God.

John 1:14

14 And the Word was made flesh, and dwelt among us, (and we beheld his glory, the glory as of the only begotten of the Father,) full of grace and truth.

Hebrews 11:3

3 Through faith we understand that the worlds were framed by the word of God, so that things which are seen were not made of things which do appear.

These specific passages give clear indication of Yeshua's existence from eternity as well as His part in creation.

In these scriptures we see Yeshua's oneness with YeHoVaH, existing as the first and the last, the Aleph and the Tov. Scripture further describes Yeshua as the Word of God, YeHoVaH's Right Hand, through Whom God created all things.

Our firm foundation, Yeshua, as spoken in Isaiah 48:12-13, holds our universe together. Hebrews 11:3 relates that faith teaches us His part in creation as the Word of God. Yet, the Bible takes us even further back in time to before the world's very creation, before the foundations came into being, God worked.

BEFORE THE FOUNDATION

Prior to laying the foundations of the earth, the Bible speaks of some amazing works of God. Among them,

God's call and assignment of Wisdom and Yeshua.

WISDOM'S CALL & ASSIGNMENT
Proverbs 8:22-26

> "**22** *YeHoVaH possessed me in the beginning of his way, before his works of old.* **23** *I was set up from everlasting, from the beginning, or ever the earth was.* **24** *When there were no depths, I was brought forth, when there were no fountains abounding with water.* **25** *Before the mountains were settled, before the hills was I brought forth:* **26** *While as yet he had not made the earth, nor the fields, nor the highest part of the dust of the world.*

Wisdom, the voice speaking in this passage, asserts that YeHoVaH called forth wisdom *before* He set in place His works of old. He brought her forth from everlasting, before the days of the earth began. As He did this, Wisdom watched the creation events.

Proverbs 8:27-31

> **27** *When he prepared the heavens, I was there: when he set a compass upon the face of the depth:* **28** *When he established the clouds above: when he strengthened the fountains of the deep:* **29** *When he gave to the sea his decree, that the waters should not pass his commandment: when he appointed the foundations of the earth:* **30** *Then I was by him, as one brought up with him: and I was daily his delight, rejoicing always before him;* **31** *Rejoicing in the habitable part of his earth; and*

my delights were with the sons of men."

As God called forth the vault of the heavens, the depths of the seas and the very mountains and hills upon the earth, Wisdom rejoiced before YeHoVaH and became His delight. Additionally, Wisdom rejoiced in her God-given assignment: *for the sons of men (all humankind) to listen to her.* Once humankind came into being and sought Wisdom, she released her qualities, which included her counsel, understanding, and strength. By Wisdom, kings reigned, and princes decreed justice, as they judged the earth.[16]

Wisdom, according to scripture, loves those who love her. She promises all who seek her *early*[17] shall find her. Wisdom leads in the way of righteousness, depositing her students upon the paths of judgment. Those who trust in her teachings find true riches and honour, the kind which endures and lasts forever. For those who love wisdom, she fills their treasure houses,[18] satisfying them with good things[19].

WHY WISDOM FIRST
Even though *Proverbs 8:27-31* identifies Wisdom as existing before the earth's foundation, one might

---

[16] *Proverbs 8:14-15.* That passage follows soon.

[17] Early implies as soon as possible, so if one notices they lack wisdom, they simply need to ask of God! *James 1:5*

[18] So, for all our getting, let us get wisdom!

[19] *Proverbs 8:14-21*

question why God desired that we know that fact. To discover the answer, think about these things:

- God set wisdom in place with a focus on the sons of men *(which include daughters, also)* [20]as she would respond to humanity's cry for help[21].
- Once Wisdom connects herself to humanity, she speaks life and truth to an individual.

Proverbs 8:14-21

"14 Counsel [is] mine, and sound wisdom: I [am] understanding; I have strength. 15 By me kings reign, and princes decree justice. 16 By me princes' rule, and nobles, [even] all the judges of the earth. 17 I love them that love me; and those that seek me early shall find me. 18 Riches and honour [are] with me; [yea], durable riches and righteousness. 19 My fruit [is] better than gold, yea, than fine gold, and my revenue than choice silver. 20 I lead in the way of righteousness, in the midst of the paths of judgment: 21 That I may cause those that love me to inherit substance; and I will fill their treasures."

From these few scripture passages, we see Wisdom

---

[20] Sons of men, as the Bible states is a generic term to comprise all humanity. This does not imply an exclusivity of others to make a "male" priority. It is simply a generic term. Please perceive it as such, here.

[21] *Proverbs 8:17.* Passage reviewed in the following paragraphs.

resides as a part of the foundation of the universe, proving to be a powerful ally to a person who calls for her. As humankind recognizes a lack of their own wisdom and seeks to find greater, more perfect wisdom, Wisdom herself comes along side to lead the seeker to truth. That truth runs towards the paths of righteousness and predictably, from that point to salvation.

YeHoVaH, therefore, called forth Wisdom for humankind. With Wisdom's help available for the asking, humanity understands God's Ways, knows the way of righteousness and how to walk in it, and learns to read, appreciate, and embrace the data of the universe as God desires its release.

Wisdom, the friend of humankind, unlocks the mysteries of the earth, making them available for use to benefit all humankind. With Wisdom, people learn how to care for the world in which they live, as well how to function in the principles God set in place for them[22]. Wisdom reveals secrets of how this earth operates, showing her children how to surpass its limitations where needed. For example, Wisdom taught humanity how to rise above the law of Gravity in order to fly.

---

[22] Gravity, the law of lift, energy, sound waves, and the like man learns to function within them, and at times, rise above them.

Wisdom, a key ingredient necessary for survival in this life on earth, God called forth and made accessible, ready to help *all who call* for her! Wisdom, one foundational aspect of earth, makes herself available for all humankind. She stands as one essential element of the universe, which streams her endless knowledge to all who seek it.

Additionally, this constant release of Wisdom, causes no problems, no distress for Wisdom. Rather, scripture relates that Wisdom delights in humankind. She rejoices in her job to help.

Proverbs 8:30-31
> ***30** Then I was by him, as one brought up with him: and **I was daily his delight**, rejoicing always before him; **31** Rejoicing in the habitable part of his earth; and my delights were with the sons of men."*
> **All those who love Wisdom[23],**
> **will also delight in YeHoVaH!**

YESHUA'S CALL & ASSIGNMENT

Securing this passage on Wisdom into a safe compartment of the mind, move forward, now. Look at another crucial element pertinent to the foundations of the world, which YeHoVaH saw fulfilled before His creation of humankind.

---

[23] While other Bible passages may not specifically declare Yeshua as Wisdom, this author believes it is so.

1 Peter 1:18-21

> *"**18** Forasmuch as ye know that ye were not redeemed with corruptible things, as silver and gold, from your vain conversation received by tradition from your fathers; **19** But with the precious blood of Christ, as of a lamb without blemish and without spot: **20** **Who verily was foreordained before the foundation of the world, but was manifest in these last times for you**, **21** Who by him do believe in God, that raised him up from the dead, and gave him glory; that your faith and hope might be in God."*

God foreordained our salvation through Yeshua, *prior to* the foundation of the earth.[24] In His infinite love and wisdom, with His foreknowledge of all things fixed in place, He realized His creation's inability to remain aligned to truth, identifying their ability to receive corruption and distain truth.   To say it differently, YeHoVaH knew the fall and its consequences as well as humankind's rejection of Him *before* He set about to even create us!   Nevertheless, YeHoVaH planned, prepared, and established His perfect plan of salvation *before* He even began to create His ultimate creation and their habitation.   Of this, the book of Revelation affirms.

---

[24] In fact, all preparations for the universe and its inhabitants rest within God's plan of Redemption for humankind.

Revelation 13:7-8

> *7 And it was given unto him to make war with the saints, and to overcome them: and power was given him over all kindreds, and tongues, and nations. 8 And all that dwell upon the earth shall worship him, whose names are not written in* **the book of life of the Lamb slain from the foundation of the world.**

IMPRESSIVE & HIDDEN, YET OPERATIVE

Knowing that God called forth Wisdom and slew the Lamb of God *before* the foundations of the world, YeHoVaH gives us two concealed principles, which indicate God's mercy, as well as certain aspects of His governing ability.

Rest assured, these two principles do not depend upon earth's existence, but upon God's immutable character. As such, these, as well as other foundational principles of our universe, remain unshakeable, and unremovable because they exist far beyond earth's control. These principles, set apart before the foundations of the world, *neither time nor sin effect.* These principles, remain as God established them: *pure, holy, and undefiled.*

Additionally, these life-giving principles point a finger of truth *directly to* the far greater government of Heaven. This government believers perceive and receive by faith. Afterwards, they long for its fullest manifestation upon the earth as their mouths declare:

"Thy kingdom come.   Thy will be done!"

As we conclude this chapter, dear one, fix these thoughts in your mind, marking the faithfulness of God's character and nature fully operative behind the scenes.   Remember, too, Wisdom continues in her consultant's role, ready and able to guide the ardent student to truth.

Yeshua declared Himself as that Truth![25]

Wisdom leads humankind face to face with Yeshua. His truth, once received, finds its fulfilment in the human heart.   Subsequently, the King of Heaven's greater government and His delightful child walk hand in hand together as friends.   This friendship grows in sweet fellowship as YeHoVaH brings to pass the effective and eventual fullness of His government and its operation upon the earth.

---

[25] *John 14: 6*

CHAPTER'S REFLECTION ♛

1 Bless YeHoVaH, O my soul. O YeHoVaH my God, thou art very great; thou art clothed with honour and majesty. 2 Who coverest [thyself] with light as [with] a garment: who stretchest out the heavens like a curtain: 3 Who layeth the beams of his chambers in the waters: who maketh the clouds his chariot: who walketh upon the wings of the wind: 4 Who maketh his angels spirits; his ministers a flaming fire: 5 [Who] laid the foundations of the earth, [that] it should not be removed for ever.

Psalm 104:1-5

In The Creator's Day 1

2

"In the beginning was the Word, and the Word was with God, and the Word was God. The same was in the beginning with God. All things were made by him; and without him was not any thing made that was made.

John 1:1-3

IN the beginning, God created the heavens and the earth.[26] Dear reader, believe this statement and you position yourself upon the solid cornerstone of truth. With this scripture (Genesis 1:1) fixed in your spirit, you hold the key which opens a large door between you and YeHoVaH.[27] Once in that door, Wisdom meets you to help you look beneath the

---

[26] *Genesis 1:1*
[27] Yeshua came to lead us to the Father, YeHoVaH.

surface works of the Almighty. In this way, you search out the deeper meaning of His actions, learning the activities operating behind the scenes.

Receiving that sight opens your eyes to recognize YeHoVaH's ability to rule in the most extreme circumstances. With that wisdom received into your being, YeHoVaH equips you and invites you to rest in His perfect control. In other words, embrace faith, dear reader, and position yourself to recognize Heaven's greater government at creation moving behind the scenes.

As YeHoVaH opens your spiritual eyes, you recognize the dynamics of the Almighty's Spirit at Creation as He moved over the face of the deep.[28] You discover a handle to unravel the mysteries[29] of the universe.

MEANT TO BE UNDERSTOOD

At creation, Heaven's governmental authority manifested through His spoken Word. This aspect of His being commanded our world into existence. In other words, His Word, as He designed it, when spoken, establishes His government. In this chapter, we explore Day One of creation, observing the Sovereign God creating. We watch as He brings chaos into order.

---

[28] *Genesis 1:2*

[29] In other words, you see what lies behind the scenes!

Looking through the open door of Genesis 1, as we discover *behind the scenes information*, we read some powerful indicators of the presence of Heaven's government at creation. As this becomes known, we learn to appreciate the ultimate builder of all things.

Hebrews 3:4
"For every house is builded by some [man[30]]; but he that built all things [is] God."

That builder, according to the book of Hebrews, identifies as God. God, like the builders of earth who wish to identify their handiwork, provided signs to His identity.

Romans 1:20
20 For the invisible things of him from the creation of the world are clearly seen, being understood by the things that are made, [even] his eternal power and Godhead; so that they are without excuse:

Here, the Apostle Paul speaks of signs which point to the earth's builder. To put these words into a contextual jargon for our day: *God made the visible world in which we live to point to the invisible world where He exists.*

In other words, all creation points to the Creator,

---

[30] KJV refers to all humankind with the word "man", not just the male gender.

Whose *invisible* world we understand through our *visible* world. From scripture's message, we hear that our world speaks like a witness attesting to its Creator. Its voice triggers in us a desire to search for truth. In doing so, the *visible things*, that which our senses know exist, point a finger to the Living God, His Power and to the Godhead.[31]

Thus, we recognize God's existence, His call, and His provided salvation as the eyewitness of earth cries out. Humankind only needs ears to hear and eyes to see! Keeping that in mind, explore Day One of creation, listening for creation's message from God.

CREATING THE HEAVENS & THE EARTH[32]
Genesis 1:1-2

> *1 In the beginning God created the heaven and the earth. 2 And the earth was without form, and void; and darkness [was] upon the face of the deep. And the Spirit of God moved upon the face of the waters.*

A surface look at Genesis 1:1-2 presents God approaching our universe *in the beginning*; however, we must understand that no universe yet existed. As God began the task of establishing our universe

---

[31] Father, Son and Spirit

[32] While scientific evidence to creation abounds, this book gives preference to spiritual truth. However, if the student desires to research the scientific data which supports creation, many books and websites exist to help aid their study.

nothing stood before Him ... not space, time, not one thing! In other words, no part of what we know, today, existed.

Thus, with that thought in mind, when scripture describes the earth without form[33], only void,[34] we recognize its emptiness, with darkness prevailing. No light whatsoever existed in the beginning. This *"nothing"* stood before God like a piece of lifeless clay awaiting the potter's hand.

Into this scene, destitute of all forms of life, entered the Spirit of the living God. He *moved*[35] upon the face of the deep, shaking or vibrating the mass of nothingness in front of Him. Amongst His activities, as He hovered over the face of the deep, He set in place the various foundational principles of the earth, energizing its energy field, forming, shaping, invigorating all aspects of the earth to meet the needs of its future inhabitants. Motivated by His plan for the existence of humankind, the Master's hand moved into motion. He began the alignment of this planet with His life plan.[36] He spoke.

---

[33] Online Bible from Strong's Concordance 08414 תֹּהוּ tohuw (to'-hoo), meaning emptiness, a place of chaos.

[34] Online Bible from Strong's Concordance 0922 בֹּהוּ bohuw (bo'-hoo), empty, waste

[35] Online Bible from Strong's Concordance 07363 רָחַף rachaph (raw-khaf'), shook, vibrated

[36] God put time and space into being in our universe. This important aspect of creation, we note here, however, this aspect of Creation, we will not explore here.

He said "light" and light appeared.

LET THERE BE LIGHT
YeHoVaH, moving into the next phase of His plan on Day One, approached the pervading darkness.

Genesis 1:3-5
3 And God said, Let there be light: and there was light. 4 And God saw the light, that [it was] good: and God divided the light from the darkness. 5 And God called the light Day, and the darkness he called Night. And the evening and the morning were the first day.

God spoke the word, "light". Immediately, light appeared in the universe, cutting through darkness. In a moment of time, by the very properties within God's eternal Word, light illuminated the heavens.

Genesis goes onto say that God called the light "Day" and the dark "Night".[37] His divine command from Heaven instigated their separation. His Word, additionally, gave them their own distinct names, declaring their separate destinies.

---

[37] ***Make note of what God named and what Adam named***. God named the day and night, as well as other things. What you name, you rule over: e.g. Parents name their children, which shows parental authority over them as they grow up beneath your wings. Note this for further study in other chapters.

Thus, by the end of the first day, out of total darkness, out of a complete void and lifeless mass, God *spoke light into being,* installing into the vault of heaven His divine order. His Word, once spoken, put an end to the sole power of darkness to bring forth a needed aspect of life, namely **light**. No longer darkness holds the universe a prisoner of its gloom. YeHoVaH's Word divided or separated the darkness, pushing it out of the way for His greater works of creation.

GOD'S WORD DIVIDES
Nothing impedes God, nor His dynamic Word. Once spoken, obedience follows. Whatever tries to stand in its way, His Word easily removes.

Hebrews 4:12
> *For the word of God [is] quick, and powerful, and sharper than any two-edged sword, piercing even to the dividing asunder of soul and spirit, and of the joints and marrow, and [is] a discerner of the thoughts and intents of the heart.*

God's Word divides! His Word separates aspects of the human heart such as thoughts, philosophies, aspiration, and the like, because the power to do so resides within the voice of the Almighty. This property of God's Word touches humankind to benefit its recipient in every way. God's Word, a powerful impact to human heart, when given freedom, changes things to align them, where necessary, with God's Will.

A COVENANT WITH DAY AND NIGHT

Here, in this passage in Genesis we identify *God's decree as He established a foundational law commanding a division between light and dark, between day and night.* God made that decree with Day and Night *a covenant*[38] and none can break that covenant! As God's Word decreed day and night into existence, He set their bounds between them. Here, in this act, we see His powerful governmental law surface.

FURTHER FOUNDATIONAL TRUTHS

As God divided the light from darkness, an *additional elementary principle* comes forth. Earlier, darkness and that without form or shape, revealed chaos. That chaos ended quickly with YeHoVaH's Word. So too, in our world, when darkness prevails, when chaotic situations arise, God's Word when spoken into it, makes a difference.

That *governmental principle*, which God utilized at creation, moves forward through time. For example, a life caught in the traps and snares of darkness cries out for help. Suddenly, the Word of truth arrives on the scene. Things change as people recognize and then accept truth.

---

[38] Jeremiah refers to this covenant of day and night in *Jeremiah 33:24-26.*

1 Peter 2:9

9 But ye [are] a chosen generation, a royal priesthood, an holy nation, a peculiar people; that ye should shew forth the praises of him who hath called you out of darkness into his marvellous light:

Those who receive salvation, God calls out of darkness into His marvellous light!   His powerful Word separates them from darkness. Now, those who exit darkness, through God's Word and power, become a chosen generation. Former captives of darkness now enjoy status as a peculiar people set aside for God. Once in the light of His kingdom, they emit the praises of the One who rescued them.

This same principle, where God moves chaos out of the way for truth to manifest, we see in the life of Daniel as he lived in Babylon. Babylon's king, Nebuchadnezzar, awoke from a powerful dream. He knew the dream held importance for him, but recalling it appeared impossible. Therefore, he demanded that his wisemen reveal both the dream and its interpretation. Failure to do that meant death to every wiseman in his kingdom, which included Daniel and his companions.

On hearing the king's edict to kill all the wisemen, Daniel, who knew his God as the revealer of secrets, presented his case before the Living God. Thus, in those chaotic hours when the King's dream taunted him, and his counsellor's feared death, Daniel prayed expecting an answer from YeHoVaH. God responded with the needed revelation.

Daniel 2:20-22

20 Daniel answered and said, Blessed be the name of God for ever and ever: for wisdom and might are his: 21 And he changeth the times and the seasons: he removeth kings, and setteth up kings: he giveth wisdom unto the wise, and knowledge to them that know understanding: 22 He revealeth the deep and secret things: he knoweth what [is] in the darkness, and the light dwelleth with him.

This dark and troubled situation disappeared into oblivion as Daniel declared to the King both the dream and its interpretation. As a result of God's light penetrating the unknown, all the counsellors lived. Daniel, the King promoted to a higher position within his own government.

LESSONS FROM MAN'S CHAOS

As God speaks, His authority rules. Darkness and chaotic situations melt. When asked, God manifests His governmental principles in situations. In Daniel's case, it manifested in God's wisdom and revelation knowledge. God-ordained and God-given wisdom stands out in this incident, showing a powerful and needed aspect of Heaven's governmental order.

God's revelation of truth, revealed by His light, exposes a far greater government than humankind constructs upon this earth.   Words from heaven, sourced in the True Light, always shatters darkness.

Matthew 4:16
16 The people which sat in darkness saw great light; and to them which sat in the region and shadow of death light is sprung up.

To those sitting in darkness comes the written or spoken Word.   Like a sharp, two-edged sword it separates the dark clouds of obscurity, making room for truth.

Situations, which seem overwhelming, chaotic, and etched with the earmarks of darkness, bow their knee to the greater government of the Living God.   God's Word causes light to manifest into the hearts of humankind, healing broken lives.   God's Word, alive and powerful, exposes, cuts off and ends the secret plans of ha satan.[39]

LOOKING BACK AT DAY ONE
God, in His Mercy set in place *major foundational principles* on Day One. His Spirit injected every needed foundational element known to man, today, or soon discovered by man, tomorrow.   Additionally, His spoken Word caused darkness to shatter and chaos to end.

---

[39] This word means adversary in Hebrew.

On this Day One of creation, YeHoVaH established a spiritual *governmental principle which believers know well*: the removal of darkness with the utterance of His Word. From creation and moving into the future, YeHoVaH made possible the recognition and utilization of His spoken word.

This governmental principle which He set in place for healing, deliverance, and salvation continues to manifest in the lives of those who wish to escape the grasp of darkness and receive eternal life!

***

CHAPTER'S REFLECTION 👑

"Yea, the darkness hideth not from thee; but the night shineth as the day: the darkness and the light [are] both alike [to thee]."

                                                        Psalm 139:12

In The Creator's Day 2 to 4

O give thanks to the Lord of lords: for his mercy endureth for ever. To him who alone doeth great wonders: for his mercy endureth for ever. To him that by wisdom made the heavens: for his mercy endureth for ever. To him that stretched out the earth above the waters: for his mercy endureth for ever. To him that made great lights: for his mercy endureth for ever: The sun to rule by day: for his mercy endureth for ever: The moon and stars to rule by night: for his mercy endureth for ever."

Psalm 136:1-9

Day 2

CONTINUING to create, YeHoVaH faces the waters. He divides them with His Word.

53

Genesis 1:6-8

"And God said, Let there be a firmament in the midst of the waters, and let it divide the waters from the waters. And God made the firmament, and divided the waters which [were] under the firmament from the waters which [were] above the firmament: and it was so. And God called the firmament Heaven. And the evening and the morning were the second day."

In this passage, we watch as YeHoVaH speaks another time. His target this time, the waters, respond to His voice. They divide as an expanse appears. Thus, God's Divine order for the heavens commences as His Word creates waters above the expanse and a portion of water, below. His work finished with the upper portion, He called it Heaven, but the lower portion He left for day three.

On day two, we recognize that by God's utterance of His Word, the properties of water changed from one form to another. At such works we marvel but we know any similar attempt by humanity means failure, unless of course the Incarnate God veiled in human flesh, camps in our midst.

John 1:14

14 And the Word was made flesh, and dwelt among us, (and we beheld his glory, the glory as of the only begotten of the Father,) full of grace and truth.

The Word, that which we see so operative at creation, chose to become flesh and walk in our midst. Such humility of a mighty God to reach inside the intricate workings of human vessel and therein plant a Divine Seed, named Yeshua.[40]

This Word of God (Yeshua), at a wedding feast in Cana,[41] changed water into wine with His command. After this miracle, His disciples obviously recognized no such power rests in humankind, and believed on Him, after this first of the miracles of Yeshua.   In Yeshua's day as well in ours, also, handling water brought numerous challenges. Rome, who ruled over Israel as Yeshua walked the earth, built aqueducts and other controls to manage water. Today, our various apparatus manage water, also, with modern equipment.

However, no one other than Yeshua demonstrated the power to divide water with a Word, and in one case, change its properties beneath His feet making it a platform upon which to walk. No other prophet or person in the universe speaks and via his voice changes water's properties. While the water parted for Moses as he led Israel through the Red Sea, and other great miracles happened within his lifespan, Moses knew God accompanied him to perform the miracles.

---

[40] Jesus
[41] *John 2:1-11*

Miracles in the life of Moses and other great prophets came not by their word, nor by their hand. It came by their faith in the One in whom they trusted and, in His ability to bring His kingdom properties actively moving in their life. Rational thought processes tell us that any ability to change the consistency of any element upon the earth *with a simple word* belongs not to humankind. Such great power belongs to the Creator and flows from the foundations of His government.

Resident in *God's Word*, which exists far above that of humankind, lives the power to instantly change the world around us. What a foundational characteristic of the governmental authority of God in our universe: the power of His Spoken Word!

Isaiah 44:6-8

> *"6 Thus saith YEHOVAH the King of Israel, and his redeemer YEHOVAH of hosts; I [am] the first, and I [am] the last; and beside me [there is] no God. 7 And who, as I, shall call, and shall declare it, and set it in order for me, since I appointed the ancient people? and the things that are coming, and shall come, let them shew unto them. 8 Fear ye not, neither be afraid: have not I told thee from that time, and have declared [it]? ye [are] even my witnesses. Is there a God beside me? yea, [there is] no God; I know not [any]."*

Day 3

Genesis 1:9-13

"9   And God said, Let the waters under the heaven be gathered together unto one place, and let the dry [land] appear: and it was so. 10 And God called the dry [land] Earth; and the gathering together of the waters called the Seas: and God saw that [it was] good.

11 And God said, Let the earth bring forth grass, the herb yielding seed, [and] the fruit tree yielding fruit after his kind, whose seed [is] in itself, upon the earth: and it was so. 12 And the earth brought forth grass, [and] herb yielding seed after his kind, and the tree yielding fruit, whose seed [was] in itself, after his kind: and God saw that [it was] good. 13 And the evening and the morning were the third day."

Once more, we watch as the Living One creates. He speaks. Waters collect into one place. Immediately, dry land[42] appears. He names the dry land *earth*, and the gathered waters *seas*.

Next, as God's Word echoes over the land, from desolate ground, YeHoVaH calls forth grasses, herbs, and fruit trees[43]. Vegetation and fruit bearing trees

---

[42] How amazing is that! Gather the waters and what is beneath surfaces as dry!

[43] Note, this sprang forth before the creation of the sun!

sprung up without hesitation, each one containing a reproductive ability within. This sustainability of life, God founded in the beginning with far reaching effects.

As He forged that which comes from the earth, He did so with life's continuance in mind. On day three, as plants and trees plentifully dot the earth, God's foreknowledge created continued sustenance for vegetation, plant, and tree matter, and for creatures not yet created[44].

In earth's formation, then, we see the manifestation of another amazing quality of God, indicating another important part of His governmental effect upon the earth, *that of provision.*

Genesis 22:14
> *14 And Abraham called the name of that place Yehovahyireh: (YeHoVaH our provider)[45] as it is said to this day, In the mount of YEHOVAH it shall be seen.*

BETWEEN DAY 3 AND 4
An amazing truth lies hidden between **Day 3 and 4.** As Day 4's events present themselves in scripture, look for that amazing message!

---

[44] Animals and humankind not yet created.
[45] Brackets added by author to explain the term. "Yehovahyireh."

With this scripture, we see the meaning of provision in God's eyes: *seeing ahead!* God's sight, focused past the immediate, embraces tomorrow. YeHoVaH plans a long timeline of existence for all His creations, which gives another indicator of our Eternal God, Who calls His creation to life. For those who trust in Him, He awaits to give His free long-range plan which extends forever. We call that plan eternal life.

Day 4

Genesis 1:14-19

> "14   And God said, Let there be lights in the firmament of the heaven to divide the day from the night; and let them be for signs, and for seasons, and for days, and years: 15 And let them be for lights in the firmament of the heaven to give light upon the earth: and it was so. 16 And God made two great lights; the greater light to rule the day, and the lesser light to rule the night: [he made] the stars also. 17 And God set them in the firmament of the heaven to give light upon the earth, 18 And to rule over the day and over the night, and to divide the light from the darkness: and God saw that [it was] good. 19 And the evening and the morning were the fourth day."

On Day 4, God speaks the creation of the sun and moon, giving them dominion over day and night. He tells us their role as signs, seasons, days, and years.

Additionally, the sun, being the greater light, rules over the day, and the moon, the lesser light, rules over the night. As usual, scripture records the end of the evening and morning the fourth day. In looking back at the two lights, the sun and moon, God's Word declares their purpose:

- as light
- as signs[46] and seasons[47], days and years.

As Signs
Signs, in Hebrew, conveys the idea of a banner. Banners serve a purpose such as our modern stop sign, or yield sign. They give information to the traveller.

As Seasons
Seasons, in Hebrew, presents the idea of a set time at which an event takes place.

HIDDEN MESSAGES
According to Psalm 19, the very message of the stars speaks to every human being who listens.

Psalm 19: 1-6
1 The heavens declare the glory of God; and the firmament sheweth his handywork. 2 Day unto day uttereth speech, and night unto night sheweth

---

[46]Online Bible from Strong's Concordance 0226 אוֹת 'owth oth sign, ensign (banner)
Online Bible from Strong's Concordance 4150 מוֹעֵד mow'ed mo-ade' appointed times, such as feasts to celebrate with God.

knowledge. 3 [There is] no speech nor language, [where] their voice is not heard. 4 Their line is gone out through all the earth, and their words to the end of the world. In them hath he set a tabernacle for the sun, 5 Which [is] as a bridegroom coming out of his chamber, [and] rejoiceth as a strong man to run a race. 6 His going forth [is] from the end of the heaven, and his circuit unto the ends of it: and there is nothing hid from the heat thereof.

God reveals His Glory to humankind, including His ultimate message of salvation. This message, God decodes to the seeker.

God places interesting messages for all those with ears to hear. Messages, such as those in the heaven, God grants humankind an ability to read, as He does other hidden messages, such as a beautiful message about His Presence. Looking back on Day 3, scripture spoke of God's creation of plant life. Not until Day 4 did God create the sun. Here a mystery arises with certain challenging questions, the answers of which bring us face to face with an amazing God, with abilities far beyond our greatest imaginations.

Of course, God never minds the questions we ask, especially when the answers reveal His greatness. So, let us ask these questions looking forward to the answers in Day 4:

**How could plant life,
which God created on Day 3,
exist without the sun?
How can the seas perform properly
without the moon[48]?**

Dear Reader,
So that message comes alive in the next chapter, ask God to
unveil this marvellous truth to you. When He does, surely
that revelation about heaven's government will delight your
heart. Assuredly, it can bring great joy to your spirit, too,
as you embrace this aspect of His Greatness!

CHAPTER'S REFLECTION

"Gird up now thy loins like a man; for I will demand of thee,
and answer thou me." "Where wast thou when I laid the
foundations   of   the   earth?   declare,   if   thou   hast
understanding. Who hath laid the measures thereof, if thou
knowest? or who hath stretched the line upon it? Whereupon
are the foundations thereof fastened? or who laid the corner
stone thereof; When the morning stars sang together, and all
the sons of God shouted for joy?"

Job 38:3-7

---

[48] Our sun sheds light for plants to grow.   Our moon's
gravitational pull generates the tidal force.

In The Creator's Day 4 Wonder

4

"All thy works shall praise thee, O YEHOVAH; and thy saints shall bless thee. They shall speak of the glory of thy kingdom, and talk of thy power; To make known to the sons of men his mighty acts, and the glorious majesty of his kingdom. Thy kingdom [is] an everlasting kingdom, and thy dominion [endureth] throughout all generations."

Psalm 145:10-13

ON Day 4, God created the sun and moon. On the day before, as already noted, He created various forms of plant life, which included trees with fruit and herbs of the ground. According to our present knowl0edge, plant growth requires five basic conditions to survive: *water, room to grow, nutrients in the soil, air, and light.*

How can plant life live if created prior to the sun?

This scenario provides a mystery to the curious mind. Mysteries once unveiled often reveal some amazing truths. To unravel the mystery and release a mystery's message, first, one must believe that the Creator desires to relay a message to the passionate student of truth. Second, one must *be that student of truth* and *receive it!*

THE MISSING INFORMATION

Let us begin with the belief that plant life did grow, as Genesis relates. We know that plants grow in *artificial lighting,* for example, so let us look for another form of light existing prior to Day 4.

On Day one, God spoke, and light came forth. Not sunlight, here, but a form of light. This light, obviously, proved adequate to provide an atmosphere for plant growth. However, before stopping here and moving on, let us consider what the witness of scripture says about life without the sun.

In the book of Revelation, the Apostle John records some amazing things, which God showed him. As we near the end of the book, where John describes the city of God, he writes:

Revelation 21:23
    23 And the city had no need of the sun, neither of the moon, to shine in it: for the glory of God did lighten it, and the Lamb is the light thereof.

Revelation 22:5

> *5 And there shall be no night there; and they need no candle, neither light of the sun; for the Lord God giveth them light: and they shall reign for ever and ever."*

Both passages relate that God's city has no need of sun, nor moon. God, Himself, lights the city.[49] God, radiant with glory dwells with humanity in that wonderful city of God, and His Presence lights it! Thus, God, present at creation, provided adequate light with His glorious Presence to sustain plant life. Believing that to be so, then, something changed on Day 4 with the creation of the sun and moon. Noting that change gives us another interesting tidbit of truth.

SUN AND MOON

First, let us recall this scripture from Chapter three,

Genesis 1:14-19

> *"14   And God said, Let there be lights in the firmament of the heaven to divide the day from the night; and let them be for signs, and for seasons, and for days, and years: 15 And let them be for lights in the firmament of the heaven to give light upon the earth: and it was so. 16 And God made two great lights; the greater light to rule the day, and the lesser light to rule the night: [he made] the stars also. 17*

---

[49] The Lamb is the light therein.

And God set them in the firmament of the heaven to give light upon the earth, 18 And to rule over the day and over the night, and to divide the light from the darkness: and God saw that [it was] good. 19 And the evening and the morning were the fourth day."

Here, on Day 4, God assigned two tasks to the sun and moon.

- *Task 1*: divide the day from the night. On Day 1, God divided light from dark and named them Day and Night, respectively. On Day 4, He shifted the continuance of day and night to the sun and moon as seen in verses 14 to 16.

- *Task 2*: Rule over day and night. On Day 4, God assigned the sun and moon "rulership"[50]. That word, rulership, clearly shows a separation of Heaven's government, as He installed the sun and moon to rule the day and night.

God, *in a governmental decision*, delegated the emulation of light to the sun to rule the day, and the moon to rule the night. This governmental installation shows us another aspect of God's form of government. *God does not dictate. He offers opportunity for people to choose or refuse His ways.*

---

[50]Online Bible from Strong's Concordance 04475 מֶמְשָׁלָה memshalah mem-shaw-law'. To rule, have dominion, government, power.

Other passages in scripture show God shared His dominion with the crown of His creation, human beings. With this aspect of God's kingdom, we see another amazing thing about Heaven's government. As He establishes the components of earth, He instituted separate governmental branches.[51] Obviously, God created both sun and moon to rule, giving all necessities to sustain their position in the heavenlies where they will remain until the command of God says otherwise[52].

AMAZING WONDER OF DAY 4

As we look at Day 4 and realize the greatness of God, some additional behaviour of God stands out. God, as seen from Day 1 onward, installed the foundational aspects of the world, *however*, He retains the rulership over them, unless He delegates it, either constantly, releasing it to the control of something else, [53] or allowing something temporarily[54] to overrule.

How God warrants the need to override *basic governmental laws of the universe* rests with Him. Foundational aspects of the universe and their constraints apply *only to humankind*. In other words,

---

[51] Heaven's government, as seen in the Tabernacle of Moses, and other places, too, shares the responsibility of Government.

[52] Scientists may say otherwise, however, God is in charge, and His hand moves, with or without our permission.

[53] Permanently with the sun.

[54] Temporarily with Joshua. *Joshua 10:12-13*

humankind lives within the foundational aspects of the universe, however, God's privilege includes overriding those basic functions.[55]

Returning to the topic of the sun and moon, seeing these as a secondary form of lighting to God's glorious Presence, interprets this way:

> *God rises higher, in every way,*
> *above all of His creation.*

YeHoVaH, greater by far than any other being, need not subject Himself within creation's parameters, restrictions, or limitations, *unless* He chooses to do so. All of creation's continuance rests within His Hands, however, His use of them He determined long ago and sustains them by His Word![56] Acknowledging this fact, encourages us to turn our face to YeHoVaH for the solution.

HEAVEN'S GOVERNMENT ABOVE EARTH'S

God expects kingdoms and nations to establish government and the citizens of that government to obey the laws and leaders, therein. However, scripture shows some cases when those governments ruled with

---

[55] Yeshua, walking on water overrode a basic element of the earth as did His multiplication of the loaves and fishes. In these cases, Yeshua functioned with the principles of the kingdom of God, which has no limitations to supply and demand.

[56] *Hebrews 1:3*

cruelty and imposed unwarranted death sentences. At such time as God willed, He overruled and thus, Heaven's government intervened.

Moses

Moses faced a most obvious and upfront issue after leaving Egypt, when he and all Israel faced a difficult situation at the Red Sea. Israel needed to move ahead to escape Pharoah and his armies. The alternative meant death at Egypt's hands. Trapped between the land mass and Pharoah's army behind them, and the Red Sea in front of them, Israel faced a problem, which no human being had the ability to solve.

Exodus 14:11-14

11 And they said unto Moses, Because [there were] no graves in Egypt, hast thou taken us away to die in the wilderness? wherefore hast thou dealt thus with us, to carry us forth out of Egypt? 12 [Is] not this the word that we did tell thee in Egypt, saying, Let us alone, that we may serve the Egyptians? For [it had been] better for us to serve the Egyptians, than that we should die in the wilderness.

13 And Moses said unto the people, Fear ye not, stand still, and see the salvation of YEHOVAH, which he will shew to you to day: for the Egyptians whom ye have seen to day, ye shall see them again no more for ever. 14 YEHOVAH shall fight for you, and ye shall hold your peace.

In the minds of the children of Israel, this life-threatening danger meant a merciless slaughter at the hands of Pharoah and his armies. Moses, however, knew Heaven's government ruled and thus, He provided salvation from Pharoah's death sentence. Israel's response need not contain fear, but trust. Be silent! Look to God and the answer comes!

God responds to the situation with a command to go forward, but where? No roads, no pathways, no bridges existed. No boats stood ready to evacuate the Israelites!

Exodus 14:15-16
> *15 And YEHOVAH said unto Moses, Wherefore criest thou unto me? speak unto the children of Israel, that they go forward 16 But lift thou up thy rod, and stretch out thine hand over the sea, and divide it: and the children of Israel shall go on dry [ground] through the midst of the sea*

Trapped with no escape possible, Israel must go forward through the Sea. Moses understood that YeHoVaH ruled above natural elements of the earth.

Heaven's government overruled that of Pharoah's!

Moses obeyed God's command and stretched his rod out over the sea. YeHoVaH caused an east wind to blow all that night, making the sea dry land[57]. By morning, with Pharoah's army pressing hard behind them, Israel's salvation manifested. They moved forward into the sea, now parted. Israel witnessed a great deliverance from Egypt. Egypt, on the other hand, experienced the hand of a just God[58] on her government as God interrupted Pharoah and his armies from their task of annihilating Israel.

Shadrach, Meshach & Abednego

In other places in scripture, God overrules unjust governments. In Babylon, for example, three companions of Daniel, named Shadrach, Meshach and Abednego faced a death sentence given by the leader of Babylon's government, Nebuchadnezzar. Their crime: *refusal to worship the gods of Babylon.*

Daniel 3: 14-18

> *"14 Nebuchadnezzar spake and said unto them, [Is it] true, O Shadrach, Meshach, and Abednego, do not ye serve my gods, nor worship the golden image which I have set up? 15 Now if ye be ready that at what time ye hear the sound of the cornet, flute, harp, sackbut, psaltery, and dulcimer, and all kinds of music, ye fall down and worship the image which I have made; [well]: but if ye worship not, ye shall be cast the same*

---

[57] Sound familiar? Check out Day 3 of Genesis! *(Genesis 1:9)*

[58] While the Bible speaks of the deliverance of the children of Israel, in this exodus experience, God's Hand judged the government of Egypt for her oppression of Israel.

71

hour into the midst of a burning fiery furnace; and who [is] that God that shall deliver you out of my hands? 16 Shadrach, Meshach, and Abednego, answered and said to the king, O Nebuchadnezzar, we [are] not careful to answer thee in this matter[59]. 17 If it be [so], our God whom we serve is able to deliver us from the burning fiery furnace, and he will deliver [us] out of thine hand, O king. 18 But if not, be it known unto thee, O king, that we will not serve thy gods, nor worship the golden image which thou hast set up."

In fury, the King sentenced Shadrach, Meshach, and Abednego to death, ordering their living bodies thrown into a fiery furnace. Heating a furnace seven times hotter, Nebuchadnezzar's top armed men threw the three Hebrews into the furnace fire. Those armed men lost their lives to the flames, but God's mighty hand saved the three children of Israel from harm.

Daniel 3:23-27

*"**23** And these three men, Shadrach, Meshach, and Abednego, fell down bound into the midst of the burning fiery furnace. **24** Then Nebuchadnezzar the king was astonied, and rose up in haste, and*

---

[59] This comment means that Nebuchadnezzar walked past the boundaries of his God-given authority when he commanded who or in this case, what people worship. This worship choice God gave to the individual, as each one gives account to God. *Acts 5:29 Then Peter and the other apostles answered and said, we ought to obey God rather than men.*

spake, and said unto his counsellors, Did not we cast three men bound into the midst of the fire? They answered and said unto the king, True, O king. 25 He answered and said, Lo, I see four men loose, walking in the midst of the fire, and they have no hurt; and the form of the fourth is like the Son of God.

26 Then Nebuchadnezzar came near to the mouth of the burning fiery furnace, and spake, and said, Shadrach, Meshach, and Abednego, ye servants of the most high God, come forth, and come hither. Then Shadrach, Meshach, and Abednego, came forth of the midst of the fire. 27 And the princes, governors, and captains, and the king's counsellors, being gathered together, saw these men, upon whose bodies the fire had no power, nor was an hair of their head singed, neither were their coats changed, nor the smell of fire had passed on them."

As the three servants of YeHoVaH entered the furnace, with them stood a fourth person, one like the Son of God. Thus, no harm came to Shadrach, Meshach, and Abednego. Freely, without chains or bounds of any kind, they walked in the flames within the furnace. As the king called the three Hebrew children to come out of the fire, the king and all his officials noted that the Hebrew children showed no sign of entering or remaining in the fire. None of their bodies, clothing, nor even the hair on their heads showed signs of being in the flames. These three servants of YeHoVaH came out of that situation without even the smell of fire on them!

GOD'S POWER ABOVE ALL THINGS

Human governments, God assigned to manage human behaviour. Religious worship, such as the object of worship, belongs to each individual. In the case of Moses and the children of the Exodus at the Red Sea, as well as the case of Shadrach, Meshach & Abednego, a life-threatening situation arose from a government that decreed laws, which fell outside of the jurisdiction that God assigns to governments.

Thus, Israel's escape from Egypt and Daniel's companions, unfairly sentenced to death by Nebuchadnezzar, escaped unjust governmental rulings. As the governments of Egypt and Babylon set about to murder some favourite worshippers of the Almighty One, He stepped in, overruled, ending the impending death, wrongly decreed.

In both Egypt and Babylon, Heaven's government overruled the unjust rulings of those, who, in their own governmental operations, directly opposed the just and righteous laws of God. Their actions deliberately defied the Creator, Who gave them life and set them to rule in their place of authority over nations. God gave them their conquests, their victories, their place of authority, and all subjects of their kingdom. Therefore, as God's precious covenant friends entered into death's grip enforced by unrighteous decrees, God arose on their behalf. YeHoVaH rescued them. His hand, His power, His might and His governmental rule in their life surpassed the rule of the earth's government. [60]

A GREATER GOVERNMENT

Throughout the scriptures, hearts rejoiced as God's Hand acted, overruling *the basic elements of the earth,* such as water as in the case of Moses, or fire as in the time of Shadrach, Meshach, and Abednego. God's ability to take charge ranks higher, far above the foundational elements of the earth. YeHoVaH's saving Hand, as we see throughout the scriptures, gave water in the desert, fed manna to two and half million people every day for forty years[61], stopped the mouths of lions[62], parted the seas and much more. His government and His ability to vindicate His own stands higher and greater. Heaven's greater government rates high as an incredible court of appeal!

---

[60] God does not intervene in every circumstance in this world when wickedness rules past their assigned borders. God did not rescue Yeshua from the cross because God had a far greater plan. It is enough for believers to understand that Heaven's government *holds the power to overrule.* To know God overruled before, gives precedence for Him to overrule again, if the situation warrants it in the mind of God.

[61] Some scholars say three million and others one million, however, in the author's research, 2.5 million seemed used most often.

[62] *Daniel 6:22 Hebrews 11:33*

DAY 4'S CALL

Day 4 of creation, *if we look behind the scenes*, calls to humankind to listen and look for *the greater government of God.* Additionally, its message, points to an ability of God to sustain life, with or without the cooperation of the normal elements which operate in the earth.

For His children, today, that means *a recognition of YeHoVaH's greatness* above our circumstances. Additionally, from the lessons of those who trusted in Him, such as Moses, we learn that *His government owns the rights to overrule that of the earth*, should the situation warrant it. *To see that happen, ensuring YeHoVaH's involvement becomes compulsory.*

Remember, cries from the children of Israel in their state of slavery arose to the supreme court of Heaven. Thus, when YeHoVaH overruled Pharoah's government, He set captives free and gave them life. His hand with the three Hebrew children in the fiery furnace proved His sovereignty over the rulership of an angry king, and spared the lives of those men, so dear to His heart.

As children of the kingdom, let us learn to understand and then grab hold of the greater workings of Heaven's government.

Let us remember the hidden lesson from Day 4!

Additionally, let us give honour and respect to YeHoVaH's authority and power to overrule laws enacted against His basic commands for man, such as commands by governments to worship other deities. Let us not limit God's response in any situation by confining Him to respond within our space or time. Rather, as His loyal and faithful children, let us acknowledge His governmental rule and His ability to rise above all things, *including the elements of this earth.* Let us not expect Him to bow to the rudimentary elements of this earth. Let us weigh all things out on His balance scale of justice and appeal to His supreme court of Law in Heaven.

Dear Reader:
Trust YeHoVaH!
His adequacy to respond and
His methods *correlate* to our appeal.
His righteous judgment, when welcomed, longed
for, and petitioned, brings to pass
***His ruling upon the earth,* as He sees fit!**

CHAPTER'S REFLECTION ♛

"That be far from thee to do after this manner, to slay the righteous with the wicked: and that the righteous should be as the wicked, that be far from thee: Shall not the Judge of all the earth do right?"

Genesis 18:25

In The Creator's Day 5

5

"Thou, even thou, art YeHoVaH alone; thou hast made heaven, the heaven of heavens, with all their host, the earth, and all things that are therein, the seas, and all that is therein, and thou preservest them all; and the host of heaven worshippeth thee."

Nehemiah 9:6

LOOKING at Day 5, once again we hear the Word of YeHoVaH bring forth life.

Genesis 1:20-23

20 *And God said, Let the waters bring forth abundantly the moving creature that hath life, and fowl that may fly above the earth in the open firmament of heaven.* **21** *And God created great whales, and every living creature that moveth, which the waters brought forth* *abundantly, after their kind, and every winged fowl after his kind: and God saw that it was good.* **22** *And God blessed them, saying, Be fruitful, and multiply, and fill the waters in the seas, and let fowl multiply in the earth.* **23** *And the evening and the morning were the fifth day."*

Speaking to the seas, God calls forth moving life within the waters[63]. Large fish such as whales, He created on Day 5, as well as every other living creature that moves about in the waters. This life came forth in great abundance, after their own kind, meaning their reproduction system fully functioned to continue on their species.

Moreover, God created fowls of the air that fly freely in the open firmament of heaven[64]. Every winged fowl, again, after their kind, also. Here, again, we see God ensuring the life, which He created, carried on, as each one had life in itself to reproduce of its own kind. Just one more reminder that God designed life to continue, for He authors all life!

Besides ensuring the continuance of life existing in our heavens, as well as in the seas, from time to time, God

---

[63] This means that on Day 3 when God called forth the plants, herbs, and fruit trees, He also brought forth whatever vegetation sea animals need for survival.

[64] As birds fly in the heavenlies, this is just one more indicator that the law of lift, and the law of gravity existed prior to day 5.

invites these creatures to help in His Divine interventions, such as in the case with Jonah and the big fish.

Jonah 1:17
"Now YeHoVaH had prepared[65] a great fish to swallow up Jonah. And Jonah was in the belly of the fish three days and three nights."

Jonah, the prophet, received a message from God to give to the people of Nineveh. Unwilling to complete his assignment, Jonah decided to run from God. Fleeing the scene, Jonah took passage on a ship going to Tarshish, a town in the opposite direction to the place where God assigned him, namely Nineveh.

Jonah 1:3-6
"3 But Jonah rose up to flee unto Tarshish from the presence of YeHoVaH, and went down to Joppa; and he found a ship going to Tarshish: so he paid the fare thereof, and went down into it, to go with them unto Tarshish from the presence of YeHoVaH. 4 But YeHoVaH sent out a great wind into the sea, and there was a mighty tempest in the sea, so that the ship was like to be broken. 5 Then the mariners were afraid, and cried every man unto his god, and cast forth the

---

[65] Online Bible from Strong's Concordance 04487 מָנָה manah maw-naw', to appoint, assign, tell what to do.

wares that were in the ship into the sea, to lighten it of them. But Jonah was gone down into the sides of the ship; and he lay, and was fast asleep. 6 So the shipmaster came to him, and said unto him, What meanest thou, O sleeper? arise, call upon thy God, if so be that God will think upon us, that we perish not."

Jonah, eager to avoid the call of God upon his life, soon discovered that he could not run from YeHoVaH. As YeHoVaH sent a wind to trouble the ship, the sailors cried out to their gods to save them. So desperate to save all on board, the shipmaster awakened Jonah. Paraphrasing his words, the shipmaster said:

"What do you mean by sleeping! Arise and call upon your God, Jonah. Perhaps He will think upon our plight and save us, so we won't all die!"

With every person onboard the ship praying, they tossed lots to see if they might receive an inkling as to the reason for the storm.

Jonah 1:7-8
"7 And they said every one to his fellow, Come, and let us cast lots, that we may know for whose cause this evil [is] upon us. So they cast lots, and the lot fell upon Jonah. 8 Then said they unto him, Tell us, we pray thee, for whose cause this evil [is] upon us; What [is] thine occupation? and whence comest thou? what [is] thy country? and of what people [art] thou?"

As the lots fall upon Jonah, he opens his mouth to speak, confessing his part in the matter.

Jonah 1:9-10
> **9** *And he said unto them, I am an Hebrew; and I fear YeHoVaH, the God of heaven, which hath made the sea and the dry land.* **10** *Then were the men exceedingly afraid, and said unto him, Why hast thou done this? For the men knew that he fled from the presence of YeHoVaH, because he had told them."*

Jonah told his story of how he ran from God. He advised the sailors that in order to calm the seas and save their lives they had but one recourse: *toss him overboard.*

Jonah 1:12
> *"12 And he said unto them, Take me up, and cast me forth into the sea; so shall the sea be calm unto you: for I know that for my sake this great tempest [is] upon you.*

Sailors, now crying out to YeHoVaH to spare them, rather than to their own gods, continued to row hard. They hoped to soon discover land. No land dotted the horizon and the storm persisted. Forced with no other choice, they followed Jonah's advice.

Jonah 1:15
> *15 So they took up Jonah, and cast him forth into the*

sea: and the sea ceased from her raging.

As seen earlier in Jonah 1:17[66], YeHoVaH, ready as always to provide an answer, prepared a great fish to care for Jonah. YeHoVaH, compassionate and caring, spared the lives of all onboard and gave Jonah a ride in a vessel to take him to his destiny, Nineveh. God did not appoint a luxury liner[67], but a fitting vessel for a stubborn prophet, who refused to obey his God.

Thus, YeHoVaH, creator of all sea life, appointed a great fish to swallow Jonah.

Inside the vessel appointed for Jonah's rescue and journey to Nineveh, the prophet repented. Afterward, God directed the fish to spew Jonah out on land, where Jonah walked on to Nineveh to declare his God-assigned message.

GOD'S RULERSHIP OVER HIS CREATION

In reviewing the many lessons from Jonah, remember we speak of an event which occurred *long after the*

---

[66] Jonah1:17 "Now YeHoVaH had prepared a great fish to swallow up Jonah. And Jonah was in the belly of the fish three days and three nights."

[67] Jonah needed the time in the dark belly of the fish to yield to the command of God on his life. Any other sort of rescue might not produce the proper result. God knows how to deal with every creature, including humans with very insistent mindsets to do things their own way!

entrance of sin and humankind's expulsion from the garden of Eden. Yet, looking at the behaviour of the large fish during the time of Jonah, we see God's creation giving us an example from which to learn.

God's Rulership Over the Large Fish[68]

In this instance, a large fish bowed to YeHoVaH's governmental order. Willingly, the fish opened its mouth and swallowed the prophet. Later, he spewed him out, unharmed, depositing him at a place close to Nineveh, where God desired the prophet to preach a message[69].

This large fish in the story of Jonah cooperated with God to the greater fulfilment of God's intended purposes. It yielded to Heaven's greater government. So too does the large sea creature scriptures describe in the book of Job:

Listen for clues as Leviathan recognizes Heaven's government and yields to it.

Job 41:1-4
  "1 Canst thou draw out leviathan with an hook? or his tongue with a cord [which] thou lettest down? 2 Canst

---

[68] We see God's hand over those sea creatures in *Job 41:1-34*. Part of it we will look at here. For more information and further study, why not read Job 41?

[69] Later, we examine that message which shows another governmental decision of God.

thou put an hook into his nose? or bore his jaw through with a thorn? 3 Will he make many supplications unto thee? will he speak soft [words] unto thee? 4 Will he make a covenant with thee? wilt thou take him for a servant for ever?

Leviathan, a large sea creature which humankind cannot harness, runs free yet makes supplications to the Creator. He even makes a covenant with YeHoVaH, and Leviathan becomes God's servant[70].

Scripture continues to describe the power of this beast, then as the passage continues, God speaks of the mightiest of men, their fears and inability to capture or tame Leviathan.

Job 41:25-34

25 When he raiseth up himself, the mighty are afraid: by reason of breakings they purify themselves. 26 The sword of him that layeth at him cannot hold: the spear, the dart, nor the habergeon. 27 He esteemeth iron as straw, [and] brass as rotten wood. 28 The arrow cannot make him flee: slingstones are turned with him into stubble. 29 Darts are counted as stubble: he laugheth at the shaking of a spear. 30 Sharp stones [are] under him: he spreadeth sharp pointed things upon the mire.

---

[70] Just like the large fish which swallowed Jonah! With God, nothing is impossible!

31 He maketh the deep to boil like a pot: he maketh the
sea like a pot of ointment. 32 He maketh a path to
shine after him; [one] would think the deep [to be]
hoary. 33 Upon earth there is not his like, who is
made without fear. 34 He beholdeth all high [things]:
he [is] a king over all the children of pride."

Remarkably, sea creatures, large and small, have the ability to recognize Heaven's government and yield to it.

God's Rulership Over the Seas

In the escape plan of Jonah's journey to Nineveh, God still ruled. We see His power over the sea, *first*, in Jonah 1:4,[71] God causes a great wind, a mighty tempest to arise in the sea. So strong was the wind and turbulent waves that the sailors feared the ship's breaking up.

Second, in Jonah 1:15[72], YeHoVaH caused the sea to cease its fierce activity, thus returning it to its previous state of calmness. Here, we see the wind and the seas, in cooperation with God, yield to the will of the Almighty to facilitate the need of the prophet as God directed.

---

[71] *Jonah 1:4* But YeHoVaH sent out a great wind into the sea, and there was a mighty tempest in the sea, so that the ship was like to be broken.
[72] *Jonah 1:15* "So they took up Jonah and cast him forth into the sea: *and the sea ceased from her raging.*"

God's Rulership Over the Situation

Jonah received a call from YeHoVaH. In mercy to Nineveh, God asked Jonah to bring a message to Nineveh. That message presented a governmental decision of YeHoVaH to bring a just judgment against Nineveh because of the people's wickedness. Jonah's call, as that of all prophets, conveys the reality of Heaven's government, and gives room for change *if repentance comes.*

Instead of obeying God's command, Jonah planned an escape. Jonah's failure to go to Nineveh meant God's judgment for their wickedness must happen. If it did, 120,000 little ones[73] under the age of reason would die. Jonah needed a direct discipline from God to help him align with God's will. His obedience would see many lives saved. Later we see, once Jonah arrived on the scene and declared his message, the people repented. God delayed His hand of judgment[74].

Jonah 3:4-10

> *4 And Jonah began to enter into the city a day's journey, and he cried, and said, Yet forty days, and Nineveh shall be overthrown. 5   So the people of Nineveh believed*

---

[73] *Jonah 4:11*   And should not I spare Nineveh, that great city, wherein are more than six score thousand persons that cannot discern between their right hand and their left hand; and [also] many cattle?

[74] In His infinite love and wisdom, God must judge sin. In a later chapter, this aspect comes under study.

God, and proclaimed a fast, and put on sackcloth, from the greatest of them even to the least of them. 6 For word came unto the king of Nineveh, and he arose from his throne, and he laid his robe from him, and covered [him] with sackcloth, and sat in ashes. 7 And he caused [it] to be proclaimed and published through Nineveh by the decree of the king and his nobles, saying, Let neither man nor beast, herd nor flock, taste any thing: let them not feed, nor drink water: 8 But let man and beast be covered with sackcloth, and cry mightily unto God: yea, let them turn every one from his evil way, and from the violence that [is] in their hands. 9 Who can tell [if] God will turn and repent, and turn away from his fierce anger, that we perish not? 10 And God saw their works, that they turned from their evil way; and God repented of the evil, that he had said that he would do unto them; and he did [it] not."

One of the best lessons, here, surfaces in the result of Jonah's obedience. God's amazing governmental rulership realigned Jonah with God's will. Additionally, it welcomed the sea and big fish to cooperate with Heaven's government to bring the situation into alignment. God's dealings with Jonah, as the result showed, aligned the prophet appropriately, and kept many souls alive. Heaven's government, and in Jonah's case, His desire to save lives, aligned the situation with His will, overturned poor choices and promoted life! Behind the scenes ruling by God made room for the salvation of many.

89

CHAPTER'S REFLECTION 👑

"Thine, O YeHoVaH, is the greatness, and the power, and the glory, and the victory, and the majesty: for all that is in the heaven and in the earth is thine; thine is the kingdom, O YeHoVaH, and thou art exalted as head above all."

1 Chronicles 29:11

In the Creator's Day 6

"What is man, that thou art mindful of him? and the son of man, that thou visitest him? For thou hast made him a little lower than the angels, and hast crowned him with glory and honour. Thou madest him to have dominion over the works of thy hands; thou hast put all [things] under his feet: All sheep and oxen, yea, and the beasts of the field; The fowl of the air, and the fish of the sea, [and whatsoever] passeth through the paths of the seas."

Psalm 8:4-8

DAY six enjoyed the calling forth of living creatures upon the earth. Yet, these creatures, as magnificent as they were, fell short of the glory of the crown of God's creation, namely, humankind.

Genesis 1:24-27

"24 And God said, Let the earth bring forth the living creature after his kind, cattle, and creeping thing, and beast of the earth after his kind: and it was so. 25 And God made the beast of the earth after his kind, and cattle after their kind, and every thing that creepeth upon the earth after his kind: and God saw that it was good. 26 And God said, Let us make man in our image, after our likeness: and let them have dominion over the fish of the sea, and over the fowl of the air, and over the cattle, and over all the earth, and over every creeping thing that creepeth upon the earth. 27 So God created man in his own image, in the image of God created he him; male and female created he them."

Immediately, after God finished creating His crown of creation, in like manner as He appointed the sun and moon to rule the Day and Night, He *appointed* humankind over creation.

Genesis 1:28-31

"28 And God blessed them, and God said unto them, Be fruitful, and multiply, and replenish the earth, and subdue[75] it: and have dominion[76] over the fish of the sea, and over the fowl of the air, and over every living thing that moveth upon the earth. 29 And God said, Behold,

---

[75] Online Bible from Strong's Concordance 03533 כָּבַשׁ kabash kaw-bash', meaning to subdue, make subservient, bring into bondage.
[76] Online Bible from Strong's Concordance 07287 רָדָה radah raw-daw', rule, have dominion, dominate, tread down, subjugate.

I have given you every herb bearing seed, which [is] upon the face of all the earth, and every tree, in the which [is] the fruit of a tree yielding seed; to you it shall be for meat. 30 And to every beast of the earth, and to every fowl of the air, and to every thing that creepeth upon the earth, wherein [there is] life, [I have given] every green herb for meat[77]: and it was so. 31   And God saw every thing that he had made, and behold, [it was] very good. And the evening and the morning were the sixth day."

Genesis reveals consistent details about creation, outlining God's order.   Here, nearing the end of Chapter 1, Genesis records a comment regarding the Almighty's next creation: *humankind*.

Genesis 1:26-27

26 And God said, Let us make man in our image, after our likeness: and let them have dominion over the fish of the sea, and over the fowl of the air, and over the cattle, and over all the earth, and over every creeping thing that creepeth upon the earth. 27 So God created man in his [own] image, in the image of God created he him; male and female created he them.

With this comment, we discover the desire of God's

---

[77] Please note: This word here means food. It could not mean meat, meaning the flesh of animals because that would mean death would have been in the garden before the fall, since one would need to kill an animal to eat their flesh. After the flood, God then instructed humankind to eat meat. Genesis 9:3

heart to position His next creation in a high position upon the earth. God prefaced no other creation with this statement, *"Let us make man in our image, after our likeness.[78]"* This statement presents a pertinent aspect of the creation upon God's heart.

Every creation YeHoVaH saw *as good*, and blessed them, desiring they increase in number and fill the earth. However, regarding humankind, after He blessed them and commanded them to multiply, He saw them as immensely good. He said:

Genesis 1:31
31 And God saw every thing that he had made, and behold, [it was] very good. [79]And the evening and the morning were the sixth day.

Yet, examining the statement before creating humankind, we recognize that God established *a precedent* above other aspects of His creation, even above the heavenlies.

Genesis 1:27
27 So God created man in his [own] image, in the image of God created he him; male and female created he them.

---

[78] Genesis 1:26 a)
[79] Bolding and italics not in original text but used here to highlight the words.

God's heart, which desired to produce a creation possessing qualities like those of His Own, revealed itself in humankind! Further definition of those qualities pokes their head as the verse continues:

Genesis 1:28-31
*"28 And God blessed them, and God said unto them, Be fruitful, and multiply, and replenish the earth, and subdue it: **and have dominion** over the fish of the sea, and over the fowl of the air, and over every living thing that moveth upon the earth."*

Dominion, in its original Hebrew language, interprets as *"radah"*[80]. This word conveys an impact of authority.

Humankind's role, God defined with one word: "dominion."

Just as God **commanded** and created the heavens and earth, governing over it, likewise He intended the crown of His creation to govern the earth. This role God further defines as He speaks a commission to His creation of humankind in the Garden.

Genesis 1:28
28 And God blessed them, and God said unto them, Be fruitful, and multiply, and replenish the earth, and

---

[80] Online Bible from Strong's Concordance 07287 רָדָה radah raw-daw', rule, have dominion, dominate, tread down, subjugate.

> *subdue it; and have **dominion** over the fish of the sea,*
> *and over the fowl of the air, and over every living thing*
> *that moveth upon the earth.*

As we look at this passage, the word "subdue" surfaces as does the word "dominion". Their Hebrew meaning helps to understand the message in God's commission to humankind. Furthermore, as we study the Hebrew origin of the words, we discover the expanse of the authority God gave to humankind.

"subdue"   KJV translated from the Hebrew word, "kabash"[81], meaning to subjugate, to make subservient, or bring into bondage.

"dominion"   KJV translated from the Hebrew word, "radah"[82].

This rule and their area of submission extended over the fish of the sea, the fowls of the air, and every living thing that moved upon the earth. After this, God installed humankind's commission, giving an order to subdue all things.

Subdue, combined with the word *dominion,* and used

---

[81]Online Bible from Strong's Concordance 03533 כָּבַשׁ kabash kaw-bash', meaning to subdue, make subservient, bring into bondage.
[82] Online Bible from Strong's Concordance 07287 רָדָה radah raw-daw', rule, have dominion, dominate, tread down, subjugate.

within the original transcripts, presents an idea of *governmental authority*. This appointment from God gave humankind a responsible position *within* Heaven's government, *which He established upon the earth at creation*.

Humankind, by God's commission and appointment, therefore, must maintain God's already established order. That order, seen from Day 1 and onward, carried a mantle of oneness with the Creator, or in simpler terms, kept in line with God's divine order.

God's humanly administrated government upon the earth must keep things in His divine order. To clarify, God's divine order in the earth *as He created it*, *must continue*. God's appointed officials, after accepting that order, watch to ensure that same order continues the way God created.

GOD'S DIVINE ORDER REVIEWED

In a quick review, we see God's Divine order as He established the universe.

- Light and Dark divided and named. *(Boundaries set up remain in place.)*
- Waters of the sea and dry land separated. *(God's established borders to remain e.g., waves of the sea do not cross over upon land creating a flood.)*
- Sun and Moon created and appointed to rule over

Day and Night. *(These correlate as God designed.)*

- Heavenly body (sun, moon, stars, etc.) for signs and seasons, days, and years. *(Remain in their order as God determined.)*

- Plant life, sea life, fowl and animal life, God ensured continuance of their life, too. *(Seed reproduced after its own kind.)* As God established the dominion order it must remain. *(Humankind above the fish, the fowl, cattle, creeping things, and all of earth's animals.)*

- God's divine order on the earth functioned perfectly; however, God put humankind in the garden to "tend" it. That tending implied watching for things which might appear out of order. In other words, God assigned Adam and his wife a commission *to watch*.

- Their God-given commission, a governmental appointment, carried with it a governmental authority. God, in the beginning, set everything in divine order, *then* He set up humankind to watch over it, to keep it as He created it.

Genesis 2:15

15 And YeHoVaH God took the man and put him into the garden of Eden to dress[83] it and to keep[84] it.

---

[83] Online Bible from Strong's Concordance 05647 עָבַד 'abad aw-bad', serve, do, dress

[84] Online Bible from Strong's Concordance 08104 שָׁמַר shamar shaw-mar', keep, observe heed, preserve, beware, watch

Here we see God took these superior specimens of His Creation, put them in a unique place and gave them their special assignment to keep the world functioning as He created it. He appointed them to subdue and govern all He delivered into their hands. This, on God's part constituted another governmental action or delegation from His kingdom, giving humankind a kingdom over which to govern.

WRAP UP
Before we close this chapter and end this first section on creation, note the governmental appointments set up in Genesis Chapter 1.

In The Heavens
When God created light, He divided the darkness. He named each one, thus giving identity to Day and Night. Later, God installed the sun and moon to govern the day and night. As He did that, He set a *powerful transition* in place, however, God never abdicated nor relinquished His control of these things. In delegating their task, *He set up a legal, governmental power backed by His government.*

At creation, we see in the heavens a definite division between light and dark. Divine order thrives as God positions heavenly bodies to govern. From their position, the earth received days, years, times, and seasons. Additionally, these heavenly bodies emitted messages to humankind, as we saw in the use of the word for signs.[85]

In The Earth

God gathered the waters, and in doing so, created dry land. He named each, designating their separate identities. God called forth sea life, sustained by life within the seas, with ability to reproduce after their kind. God created humankind. He set them in a position of dominion, decreeing to them a governmental appointment with a definite job description.

That commission, with similar earmarks to that of the sun and moon, functioned as a legal entitlement to the earth, entirely backed by Heaven's government. What decisions humankind made in that garden of Eden, at the expression of their word[86], became law.

After the season of creation ends, defining lines exist, showing the uniqueness of God's order:
- Between light and dark
- Between heavens above and earth below
- Between day and night
- Between sea and dry ground
- Between sea life and animal life

---

[85] Online Bible from Strong's Concordance 0226 אוֹת 'owth oth, ensign, sign.

[86] Remember, God created humankind in His image!

- Between animal life and human life

Creation functions as God designed it ... *to last*. We see this as reproduction systems exist to further life in the seas and on the dry land. All these show themselves as completely efficient for life to continue, *after their own kind*. Lastly, we see humankind, the crown of God's creation, receiving their governmental appointment and the associated authority needed to watch, keep, and subdue the earth.

CHAPTER'S REFLECTION

"For I know that YeHoVaH is great, and that our Lord is above all gods. Whatsoever YeHoVaH pleased, that did he in heaven, and in earth, in the seas, and all deep places. He causeth the vapours to ascend from the ends of the earth; he maketh lightnings for the rain; he bringeth the wind out of his treasuries."

Psalm 135:5-7

COURSE 202

Heaven's Greater Government

יְהֹוָה

SECTION 2:
RULING IN THE EARTH

In the Creator's Sabbath

7

"Who is like unto thee, O YeHoVaH, among the gods? who is like thee, glorious in holiness, fearful in praises, doing wonders? Thou stretchedst out thy right hand, the earth swallowed them. Thou in thy mercy hast led forth the people which thou hast redeemed: thou hast guided them in thy strength unto thy holy habitation."

Exodus 15:11-13

AFTER God created the entire system of our galaxy, the world in which we live, He rested from creating. In other words, that which God desired to create, He finished. He deemed nothing left undone that needed to be done regarding the habitation He created for humankind.

Genesis 2:1-3

1 Thus the heavens and the earth were finished, and all the host of them. 2 And on the seventh day God ended his work which he had made; and he rested on the seventh day from all his work which he had made. 3 And God blessed the seventh day, and sanctified it: because that in it he had rested from all his work which God created and made.

On that seventh day, which began like every other day in the evening, He ended His creation work and rested. Many believers over the centuries picture God in a position of rest, not moving about, doing absolutely nothing. However, to think this does the passage injustice, as Scripture, in its original language, makes it clear that God rested or ceased his labours of creation. Yet, God still works in ways other than creation!

Yeshua, as He did a miracle on the Sabbath, said this, when certain Jewish leaders rebuked Him:

John 5:17

17 But Jesus answered them, My Father worketh hitherto, and I work.

Jewish leaders perceived the action of Yeshua's healing miracle as work, and thus, in their religious minds, Yeshua violated the Sabbath when no person should work. In response to their accusation, Yeshua declares that God, His Father, always works, and He works also. This message, strong and vocal out of the mouth of Yeshua, makes it clear that His Father, the Creator, actively involved Himself with the affairs of humankind. While YeHoVaH rested from His acts of creation, He neither forsook nor abandoned humankind. He worked, actively involved in what took place in the lives of humankind.

Yeshua, knowing Jewish leaders invented teachings not found within the scriptures, challenged the religious authorities of His day to align their thinking with the Word of God. Scripture both teaches and shows God's enthusiasm and active participation in the affairs of humankind, no matter the day of the week! It does not show Him as apathetic.

According to scripture, while God, after creation, ceased from working in the aspect of creation, He continued to work in the many dealings of humankind. A quick review of just Genesis shows God active in the lives of humankind, some that followed Him and some that did not:

- God addressed Cain's heart before Cain slew Abel. *(Genesis 4:7)*
- He appeared to Abraham and called him out of idolatry to give him a place to live as a separate entity unto God. *(Genesis 12:7; Acts 7:2)*
- He spoke with Hagar when she ran from Sarah, her mistress. He gave her advice and help.

(Genesis 16:7-9)

Many more incidents from Genesis to Revelation, relate God's interest in humankind. Each one recounts how God, the Creator, actively moved within our universe, watching, caring, speaking, and looking for places to show Himself strong.[87]

We do God great injustice if we perceive Him sitting down, uninvolved, and uninterested in the affairs of humankind. We honour Him, when we recognize His loving hand operative in our universe, our nations and our individual lives and seek His help!

A VERY DIFFERENT DAY

Throughout Genesis Chapter 1, scripture describes the activity of 6 creation days. It ends the days with these words "the evening and the morning". With these words, the author clarifies that each day began in the evening, and then, the following evening, the next day began. Thus, we know that each day had a beginning and an ending.

However, when it comes to Day 7, scripture reads differently. It tells us the finished works of the heavens and earth and all the host of them. Then, it announces the arrival of Day 7, but never concludes the day. Since

---

[87] *2 Chronicles 17:9* This invitation on God's part to man shows God's desire for man to seek His help for all situations, especially those extremely difficult ones.

scripture never officially ends Day 7 as it did other days, God presents us with a profound message.

DAY 7 NEVER ENDS

As we unlock the message in Day 7, remember on Day 4 the 24-hour day began. Thus, God's first message regarding Day 7's continuance presents a theoretical or prophetic message which scripture interprets in other passages. One such passage comes alive in the words of Yeshua:

John 9:4
> *"I must work the works of him that sent me, while it is day: the night cometh, when no man can work."*

To understand Yeshua's statement and just how it aligns with Day 7's continuance, one must *embrace two things:*

- *Yeshua's purpose on earth*
- *God's plan for all humankind*

Yeshua's purpose for coming, we discover in His name, which interprets as **salvation**. God's purpose for all humankind, also, sums up in the word: **salvation**. To make a long story short, God's plan for earth lies within the parameters of one word:

REDEMPTION

To summarize, redemption's plan began *before* God created time or space. Creation Day 1 to 6 shows creation activities. Day 7 shows creation finished. God rests from His creation, then blesses the day and sets it apart, above all other days. As the Bible continues to record, it moves immediately in the genealogy of the heavens and earth.

Genesis 2:4

> *4 These [are] the generations of the heavens and of the earth when they were created, in the day that the YeHoVaH Elohim made the earth and the heavens,*

Next, a very important event becomes evident. On day 7, moving into Chapter 3 of Genesis, Adam disobeyed God. Sin entered[88] and[89] death's reign began.[90] Still, within the framework of Day 7, God immediately presents His redemption plan[91]. God's redemption plan awaited Adam and Eve's acceptance and continues to wait from Genesis onward, as person after person embraces the redemption which God planned for them.

---

[88] While God never created humankind to know good and evil, His foreknowledge showed Him that would happen.

[89] *Romans 5:12*

[90] *Romans 5:14*

[91] *Genesis 3:15* records the first message of the gospel. For this reason, scholars call *Genesis 3:15* the protoevangelium. (The gospel as presented by God to humankind.)

So, in our world while the 24-hour cycle of day and night repeats itself, God's extension of His redemption plans continues until every person who would accept it, does. In this light, Day 7 continues until day gives way to night. Night comes when no person left alive wishes to receive God's redemption plan.

John 9:4 shows that Yeshua understood this concept. He worked with His Father within *daylight hours*, however, He warned the night soon comes when no human works. In other words, Yeshua came and worked in the light, however, He warned His disciples that night comes, or when Day 7 completes, redemption's invitation ends.

When the 7th Day ends, God creates a new heaven and earth. That begins Day 8.

Revelation 21:1
   "And I saw a new heaven and a new earth: for the first heaven and the first earth were passed away; and there was no more sea."

Within this 7th Day principle, we see valuable aspects of Heaven's government. *First*, it shows us that God works in a different timeframe than the 24-hour schedule of humankind. To be exact, God lives *outside of time*. God's existence before creation, as well as this extension of Day 7, makes that fact very clear.

Second, God set Day 7 apart, above all other days. As He did this, He reenforced the most important reason for humankind's existence upon the earth: redemption. Also, He emphasizes an important aspect of the faith: to rest on and in His special day!

PRINCIPLE OF REST

Looking at the 7th Day as the day of Redemption, additionally we note that God rested. Redemption and rest connect!

Hebrews 4:4-10

> *"4 For he spake in a certain place of the seventh [day] on this wise, And God did rest the seventh day from all his works. 5 And in this [place] again, If they shall enter into my rest. 6 Seeing therefore it remaineth that some must enter therein, and they to whom it was first preached entered not in because of unbelief: 7 Again, he limiteth a certain day, saying in David, To day, after so long a time; as it is said, To day if ye will hear his voice, harden not your hearts. 8 For if Jesus had given them rest, then would he not afterward have spoken of another day. 9 There remaineth therefore a rest to the people of God. 10 For he that is entered into his rest, he also hath ceased from his own works, as God [did] from his."*

Hebrews makes clear reference to the Day 7, as well as the importance of entering our rest. Again, redemption and rest connect. It begins by first, setting aside the day of rest, then learning from its principle.

KEEPING THE 7TH DAY

Believers keep the Sabbath day in two ways: naturally and spiritually.

NATURALLY, as people rest from their physical labours. Most of those hours included working for their livelihood, caring for family matters and taking care of the things set before them daily. When the Sabbath[92] arrives, this type of labour gives way to a retreat from the normal. On the Sabbath, believers, therefore, receive opportunity to grow stronger in their faith, or honour God for His mighty hand functioning in their lives or those of loved ones, or enjoy better fellowship with the One Who created them.

A Sabbath rest provides an open door to leave behind the labour of the six days prior, to gaze with a greater intensity into the spiritual things of God. On a Sabbath rest, as believers walk away from their normal, mundane tasks, they seize the opportunity to enter an open door to draw nearer to God. This day allows for a change of activity from *the normal* to discover more about the Creator!

SPIRITUALLY, as a person embraces God's redemption, they realize that He did it all through Yeshua. No person brings to God anything towards their redemption, only the gift of Salvation suffices!

---

[92] Some people celebrate their Sabbath apart from the actual 7th day. No matter the day, the principle of the Sabbath applies!

That gift humankind receives free and clear[93]. Thus, when understood, the recipient ceases from works to complete their own salvation and accepts the free gift. Afterward, communication with God continues from that place of rest.

In other words, as believers receive salvation, they enter their rest. Like God, they cease from works *leading to redemption*. Afterward, just as God continued to take an interest in His creation, communicating with them and blessing them, so, too, do the redeemed continue to embrace their communication with God.

GOD'S REST & HEAVEN'S GOVERNMENT

God's active days of creation emphasize that both He and His government generate life. We see this life as He spoke everything into being from day one when He said, *"Let there be light"*, and onward to the close of the sixth day. On the seventh day, a greater extension of His abundant life manifests as He rests, then blesses and sets the 7th day apart.

On this day, as **God entered His rest**, by His example He invites the ones created in His Image to do as He does. His arms extend wide open to the crown of His creation, **humankind, to enter His rest, too.** This 7th day, which began after the completion of all creation, remains until God creates a new heaven and earth.

---

[93]To understand more about Salvation, turn to the Appendix.

This aspect of God's presentation to humankind demonstrates another foundational principle of Heaven's government, namely, *to function within the aspects of Heaven's government, His people must learn to rest.*

Believers who learn to understand the Sabbath rest and step into His rest for their salvation, embrace life as God designed it: *Resting in His finished works.* This principle applies to enter and receive God's provided redemption *and* moves past that open door of salvation to extend in every direction of kingdom activity.[94]

As God rested, as He set apart the 7th Day, which prophetically continues onward, we embrace a key to walking within the higher order of Heaven's government. His kingdom operates on finished principles:

- God told Moses that he would know God sent him into Egypt, when the people which he brought forth would serve Him on that mountain.[95] God saw the work was done before Moses left. Moses only need follow.
- God told Joshua a plan to destroy Jericho, a plan

---

[94] Moses, Joshua, and the saints of old entered that rest and did their works from within that position of rest. Such is the satisfied state of one who understands this principle of Heaven's greater government!

[95] *Exodus 3:12*

115

which included blowing trumpets and waiting on God. As the ark went around the city, God caused the walls to fall and gave them the city. God saw the work as done! Joshua merely followed[96].

- Yeshua told His disciples that whatsoever they bind[97] on earth, God already bound that thing in heaven, and whatsoever they loose[98] on earth, God already loosed that thing in heaven[99].

Heavens' greater government operates with principles far surpassing those of the earth! Rest, just one of the principles of that government, when learned and practiced, aligns God's people so they function for God and with God.

What a way to live!

---

[96] *Joshua Chapter 5 and onward*
[97] Meaning restrained or refused to allow to operate
[98] Give freedom to operate.
[99] *Matthew 16:19 (Greek term used applies work already done.)*

REDEMPTION'S TIMELINE
(PROPHETIC VIEW)

PRE WORLD	Pre- Creation	Lamb of God slain
Evening & Morning	Day 1 to 3	Light (Plus creation's activities)
Evening & Morning	Day 4 to 6	24 hour Day plus creation activities
Prophetic Day Starts	Day 7	Prophetic Day of Rest Begins (This day continues from 1st Adam until the 8th day begins)
Post Present World	Day 8	Creation of New Heaven & Earth

CHAPTER'S REFLECTION 👑

"There remaineth therefore a rest to the people of God. For he that is entered into his rest, he also hath ceased from his own works, as God did from his.   Let us labour therefore to enter into that rest, lest any man fall after the same example of unbelief."

Hebrews 4:9-11

In The Creator's Crown of Life

8

"In thee, O YEHOVAH, do I put my trust; let me never be ashamed: deliver me in thy righteousness. Bow down thine ear to me; deliver me speedily: be thou my strong rock, for an house of defence to save me. For thou art my rock and my fortress; therefore for thy name's sake lead me, and guide me. Pull me out of the net that they have laid privily for me: for thou art my strength. Into thine hand I commit my spirit: thou hast redeemed me, O YeHoVaH God of truth."

Psalm 31:1-5

CONTINUING in Day 7, Genesis Chapter 2 lists the genealogy of creation and presents us with a personal encounter with humanity's first couple happily within their haven of Eden. However, as Genesis 2 unfolds, we learn that life within Eden contained a restriction:

Genesis 2:17

> *17 But of the tree of the knowledge of good and evil, thou shalt not eat of it: for in the day that thou eatest thereof thou shalt surely die.*

Living within this magnificently created world, this first couple[100], having received their commission[101], operated in their governmental function to care for their world and the creatures within it. In the training ground of Eden, the crown of creation learned to walk in their governmental call, keeping God's established order within their universe. Their watchful eye, according to their assignment, surveyed for things which might function outside of the way God created it. If they perceived that happening, they must subdue it to realign it with God's divine order. In this way they govern the earth, fulfilling the command of God to have *dominion*.

**To fulfill their governmental role,
they must subdue.[102]**

A SITUATION TO SUBDUE

One day, as Genesis 3 relates, something out of God's established order manifested in Eden.

---

[100] God named Adam. Until after the fall when Adam named Eve, scripture addresses her as "woman". This distinguishes her from before the fall and after. This book follows that same pattern of distinction.

[101] *Genesis 1:28*

[102] *Genesis 1:28*

Genesis 3:1-5

"Now the serpent was more crafty[103] than any beast of the field which YeHoVaH God had made. And he said unto the woman, Yea, hath God said, Ye shall not eat of every tree of the garden? And the woman said unto the serpent, We may eat of the fruit of the trees of the garden: But of the fruit of the tree which is in the midst of the garden, God hath said, Ye shall not eat of it, neither shall ye touch it, lest ye die. And the serpent said unto the woman, Ye shall not surely die: For God doth know that in the day ye eat thereof, then your eyes shall be opened, and ye shall be as gods, knowing good and evil."

A serpent began to speak to the woman.[104] In his address, he accused God of evil intentions, not having the couple's best interest at heart.[105] Then, the serpent urged the woman to eat the forbidden fruit. She ate and gave the fruit to her husband, who ate, too.

To eat of this tree, as God related, meant death, however, according to the serpent's words, eating meant wisdom. Adam and his wife having eaten[106] the

---

[103] KJV says "subtil", (not subtle) however, since we do not use this word, today, the author inserted another word which means the same thing as KJV subtil.

[104] "woman" in Hebrew comes from the word fire. Adam's wife, a flaming fire, a strong and mighty warrior, shared the dominion with him.

[105] Does not want you to know good or evil.

[106] Please note: Disobedience to the command of God caused the problem. Eating the fruit, as it entered the stomach did not defile them! *Mark 7:15*

fruit, discovered which voice related truth. Suddenly, the couple's eyes opened. Immediately, shame for their naked bodies gripped them. To hide their shame, they made aprons *(חֲגוֹר[107] loin coverings)* for themselves. Later, when "they heard the voice of God walking in the garden"[108], they hid from Him.

GOD'S COURT OF LAW CONVENES
In Eden, after the couple disobeyed the command of God, Heaven's government reveals itself. This couple, who chose to disobey God, now must give an account to the supreme ruler of the universe. God, in His mercy, calls them out from their hiding place. Then, He gives them opportunity to explain their behaviour. God approaches Adam to present their defence. Their free choice, a gift within the governmental setting of God's kingdom, required accountability.

Thus, in Genesis 3, *after the erroneous choice of disobedience,* we have a courtroom scene. As Adam gives accountability for his actions, his defence sourced the problem to the woman and to God, Who

---

There is nothing from without a man, that entering into him can defile him: but the things which come out of him, those are they that defile the man.

[107] Online Bible from Strong's Concordance 02290 חֲגוֹר chagowr khag-ore'

[108] This wording may seem strange; however, this is a direct quote of KJV *Genesis 3:9.* Its meaning shows that they heard *the voice of God* walking. Interesting phraseology, most likely referring to the Word of God.

He gave to him. When given opportunity to defend herself, the woman[109] blamed the serpent. In her mind, the serpent kept his ulterior motives hidden, therefore he caused the problem due to his deceptive behaviour.

After hearing the defence of the woman, God closes the case. No opportunity for defence comes to the serpent[110]. Rather, God, the Judge of all the earth and still its Supreme Ruler, makes a governmental decision and addresses the serpent. As God spoke His judgment, He subjugated the serpent to a subservient role, forever. With God's judgment given to the serpent, He did what Adam and the woman failed to do: *subdue the serpent*.

Adam and his wife, who operated the current earth's government, failed in their task. However, Heaven's greater government, did not. This first couple watched the Supreme Ruler release a fair and righteous judgment upon the serpent and then upon them. Their judgment, which included exile from the Garden, came, but not before God presented a plan to counteract the problem, which resulted from their

---

[109] Remember: Eve, at that time, did not have a name. That name came later.

[110] As the serpent entered the garden to tempt the couple, he trespassed his boundaries. With intentions to directly oppose Heaven's government on the earth and the authority given to the human couple, he acted. Those premediated, predetermined actions, in direct opposition to God and His government, meant the serpent met with God's full measure of judgment.

disobedience.

DEATH NOW REIGNS[111]

Disobedience to God's Word, while no surprise to God, hit hard against all His Creation.[112]   After the forbidden fruit event, *death* entered the world. Death's first kill manifested quickly.   God's crown of creation, intended for eternal life, immediately became subjected to death. In mercy, God presented His plan to restore humankind in their relationship with Him.

Genesis 3:15
   15 And I will put enmity between thee and the woman, and between thy seed and her seed; it shall bruise thy head, and thou shalt bruise his heel.

God's decision to *remove death's sting* and *restore life* meant a divine intervention through His power, ruling above the *new natural* course of life. Not through man's seed, *where death entered* the world, but through the woman's seed.[113]   YeHoVaH's promise entailed the birth of a human being above the natural way He created, from *the seed* of *the woman*[114]. This seed, as God

---

[111]*Romans 5:11-14*

[112] Death entered the universe and affected it in every way. *Romans 8:22* speaks of all creation groaning.

[113] God created creatures to reproduce their own kind, thus after the fall, Adam brought forth his own kind: *the disobedient.* God promised a seed from outside Adam's seed, an obedient one born of a woman.

[114] One can see Heaven's greater governmental order in Yeshua's

called it forth, *bridges the divide* between sin's penalty, *death*, and God's design for humankind, *eternal life*.

Earlier, through the words of the serpent, Adam and his wife heard a promise and believed it: *"Ye shall not surely die: For God doth know that in the day ye eat thereof, then your eyes shall be opened, and ye shall be as gods, knowing good and evil"*. Now, God related His promise backed by His integrity: *"And I will put enmity between thee and the woman, and between thy seed and her seed; it shall bruise thy head, and thou shalt bruise his heel."* [115]

Adam and his wife believed the serpent's words and stepped towards that promise, thus *opening the door to death*.   Later, as God presented the message of His promised Deliverer, they believed, *opening the door to life*.   However, between Eden and the manifested Promised One, God removed Adam and Eve from the Garden.

ANOTHER INFLUENCE ON EARTH
As humankind moved out of Eden to the remaining parts of the earth, death, which entered the world through humankind's choice, now reigned. Death's influence touched the whole universe. Misalignment with God's perfect order manifested on all fronts[116].

---

birth!

[115] *Genesis 3:15*

[116] All creation groaned, *Romans 8:22*, shows the depth of the effect of sin. A later chapter explains this further.

Impacted by death, earth no longer responded the same. An entire planet, day by day, showed the effect of sin, as it continued out of synchronization with God. Until death loses its victory, the earth and all in it remains out of alignment, however, God's promise to humankind in the Promised One brings victory over death, when God renews the earth. So, while death reigned, life lay within the grasp of humankind by faith in the promise of *Genesis 3:15*

Humanity's responsibility to govern the earth, went with Adam and Eve as they left the garden.

Genesis 3:16-19
> *"16 Unto the woman he said, I will greatly multiply thy sorrow and thy conception; in sorrow thou shalt bring forth children; and thy desire [shall be] to thy husband, and he shall rule over thee." "17 And unto Adam he said, Because thou hast hearkened unto the voice of thy wife, and hast eaten of the tree, of which I commanded thee, saying, Thou shalt not eat of it: cursed [is] the ground for thy sake; in sorrow shalt thou eat [of] it all the days of thy life; 18 Thorns also and thistles shall it bring forth to thee; and thou shalt eat the herb of the field; 19 In the sweat of thy face shalt thou eat bread, till thou return unto the ground; for out of it wast thou taken: for dust thou [art], and unto dust shalt thou return."*

Adam and his wife, originally set within the Garden to keep the garden, must continue operating in their governmental mantle. Since sin and death entered, that job increased in difficulty, yet the command *to subdue* remained unaltered.

FAMILY GOVERNMENTAL ORDER

Prior to the expulsion from the garden of Eden, God reenforced family order. In the garden, Adam and Eve operated as co-regents. Nevertheless, we see from Genesis 3 that even though Eve handed Adam the forbidden fruit, she was deceived by the serpent but Adam *deliberately disobeyed.*

1 Timothy 2:14
14 And Adam was not deceived, but the woman being deceived was in the transgression.

That role of Adam's accountability to God, continued after the fall, and Eve, as well, must continue to give an account for her actions.

Genesis 3:16
"16 Unto the woman he said, I will greatly multiply thy sorrow and thy conception; in sorrow thou shalt bring forth children; and thy desire [shall be] to thy husband, and he shall rule[117] over thee."

"Rule" in Hebrew, in this verse above, comes from the

---

[117] Online Bible from Strong's Concordance 04910 מָשַׁל mashal maw-shal' rule, have dominion.

same word used in Genesis 1:28 which shows *governmental authority*. Simply put, God reenforced the governmental role given earlier to humankind. As before, the governmental leader brings accountability to God, and here, it is well noted that the woman gives accountability to Adam.

When God appointed Adam as family head, He used the same word as in the commission of humankind to "rule" the earth. God did not add the word, *subdue*. With the absence of this word, God made a clear statement regarding the principle which He set up over families.

A family head exists for reasons of accountability. Male dominance or subjugation of women plays no role here. God sets the boundaries for families with the husband as the person of accountability. Eve, who *never lost her equality with Adam*, subjected herself as directed by God to Adam's governmental position, and respected it[118].

Adam, as seen after the garden and every father, thereafter, watched over their families, knowing that God held them accountable for their family's behaviour. Wives and children gave account to their

---

[118] *Ephesians 5:33* "Nevertheless let every one of you in particular so love his wife even as himself; and the wife *see* that she reverences *her* husband."

husband/father. Sitting in a governmental role, then, the father dispensed judgment for those who disobeyed.

In this we see God's
governmental family order. [119]

AN ACCOUNTABILITY PRINCIPLE
As civilization progressed, family government continued evolving to stretch to heads of tribes, then to those of cities and nations. While humankind added their own ideas to government, often supressing the people, God's accountability principle never changed.

Any person in a governmental role, within or without the home, the Biblical model of leadership holds a responsibility to rule as God rules: *with love, compassion, forgiveness, and mercy.* Authority, as scripture teaches throughout the bible, outlines with the right to rule, however, as seen in the garden, the priority shows itself to be one of service to others[120].

As always, an accountability to God *in all aspects of that government* existed from leader to followers. We see this principle throughout the scriptures no matter who

---

[119] This is a simplistic view. To show more moves into another aspect "man's government" which is not the theme of this book.
[120] While Adam and the woman had God's commission to rule, their command to "tend" the garden suggested their service. As they serve, and as they see things out of alignment, they bring it back into God's order.

sat in leadership. We see it in the lives of some notable men such as Moses and Joshua. It manifests in the book of Judges in a woman named, *Deborah*[121].

When we arrive at the teachings of Yeshua, we hear Him reemphasize what He knew as truth:

Mark 10:44-45

"44 And whosoever of you will be the chiefest, shall be servant of all. 45 For even the Son of man came not to be ministered unto, but to minister, and to give his life a ransom for many."

Later, we hear of powerful Apostles, among them a women named Junia.[122] Also, Priscilla, a pastor, sits in a place of authority within the setting of the New Covenant. Their position in their assembly as given by God, gave them the right to exercise that authority, and a responsibility to do so with accountability to God.

In fact, no matter the place of authority or the gender which occupies it, whether in a church setting or out of it, it seems that God desires all leaders who exercise their governmental control to embrace their responsibility to bring the knowledge of the Creator and His character to others. Granted, those who know God should do a better job, but even those who do not know Him still account to Him for their actions! Ruling

---

[121] An obvious given that God has no problem with a woman rising to power in His Name to Judge His people.
[122] A woman Apostle in Paul's day.

in places of authority, at any level and in any situation, means both *accountability* to God *and service* to those of whom God has given them charge. [123]

A RENEWED GOVERNMENT

As Genesis 3 closes, we see Adam and Eve leaving the garden, dressed in garments God made for them.[124] With God reemphasizing their appointment as governors (care givers) and with the death factor they invited, God renewed their governmental appointment over the earth. Governing or keeping watch over the earth, from the expulsion from the garden onward, turned out to be a more intense experience than earlier. To walk in this new world order where death reigned, *and to attempt to align it as close as possible to the divine order in which God created it,* numerous challenges existed. Their journey to triumph over sin and death lay within the plan of redemption, which God laid out for them and their seed. His plan of mercy stood available to them and their seed if, by faith, they embraced it.

---

[123] Take note that God gave Assyria charge over Northern Israel, and He judged them, too, for their mistreatment of Israel. Same too with Babylon. God gave them charge of Judah and Jerusalem and held them accountable for their treatment of the people.

[124] An animal died to provide those garments. Bible scholars believed God slayed a lamb and thereby showed them the acceptable sin offering. Adam and Eve accepted God's plan of redemption, as shown earlier in this book.

HEAVEN'S GREATER GOVERNMENT

Adam and Eve left the garden to establish the first human government *outside of the garden.* They attended to their own personal needs, and that of their family, however *death reigned over them.* Nevertheless, a far superior government still operated on their behalf, where God reigned. His government stood from the beginning and onward, as an administration of *life,* unaltered and unaffected by sin and death.

CHAPTER'S REFLECTION ♛

"When I consider thy heavens, the work of thy fingers, the moon and the stars, which thou hast ordained; What is man, that thou art mindful of him? and the son of man, that thou visitest him? For thou hast made him a little lower than the angels, and hast crowned him with glory and honour. Thou madest him to have dominion over the works of thy hands; thou hast put all things under his feet: All sheep and oxen, yea, and the beasts of the field; The fowl of the air, and the fish of the sea, and whatsoever passeth through the paths of the seas. O YEHOVAH our Lord, how excellent is thy name in all the earth!"

Psalm 8:3-9

To all with ears to hear,

Heaven's greater government stands as a government of
LIFE.

Humankind's entrance to that Government and *its consistent operation to overcome death in our life* depends upon *our ability to enter His spiritual Sabbath rest!* We do this by faith as we look to Him and trust in the finished works of the Creator including that works which brings us Eternal life!

In The Creator's Call of Choice

9

"The heathen are sunk down in the pit that they made: in the net which they hid is their own foot taken. YeHoVaH is known by the judgment which he executeth: the wicked is snared in the work of his own hands. Higgaion. Selah. The wicked shall be turned into hell, and all the nations that forget God. For the needy shall not alway be forgotten: the expectation of the poor shall not perish for ever. Arise, O YeHoVaH; let not man prevail: let the heathen be judged in thy sight. Put them in fear, O YeHoVaH: that the nations may know themselves to be but men. Selah."

Psalm 9:15-20

FROM the fall of humanity, onward, with the earth of out synchronization with God's original design, much changed.[125]   Instead of the earth's original processes of life and peace, an enmity arose between God and man due to the entrance of sin and death. While God revealed His redemption plan to deal with the sin factor and bridge the gap between God and humankind, other factors affected the earth and its major function.

Paul, the Apostle, put it this way in his exhortation to the Romans.

Romans 8:22
  "22 For we know that the whole creation groaneth and travaileth in pain together until now."

Paul's statement focuses on a future time when God's promise of restoration comes to pass. At that time, victory swallows death[126] and life flows throughout the entire earth once more, *just as it* did *prior to* the entrance of sin and death. Until that day, all creation groans or looks forward to it, just like a pregnant woman groans as her time comes to receive new life into the earth.

In other words, Paul teaches that all of creation, which means our entire universe and all within it, groans in agony, gripped with birth pains like an expectant

---

[125] God's consistent factor in creation being life, collided with death which entered, and thus, the earth became out of synchronization.
[126] *Hosea 13:4, 1 Corinthians 15:55-57*

mother waiting for the resurrection of the body, or the divine order of God returns one hundred percent to the earth. Until that day, (the 8th day), all creation awaits the dynamic change resurrection power brings. Creation groans for the absence of such power today, and anxiously awaits for its manifestation in the future.

In the meantime, the earth walks through its existence with many modifications due to sin. We hear of death's entrance, and not foo far into Genesis we hear of the first murder, which greatly affected the earth.

CAIN AND THE GROUND
In Genesis 4, God presents the life of two brothers, Cain, and Abel. Cain, the first-born son of Adam and Eve, tills the ground. Abel, the second born son, tends sheep. Cain receives an abundant harvest from the ground and brings an offering to YeHoVaH. Abel raises sheep, at which task he excels. Each son of Adam brings an offering to God.

Abel brings a sheep offering, acknowledging his need of God and professes his faith in the redemption plan of God. God accepted the offering. However, Cain, while he brought forth a beautiful grain offering, neither acknowledged his need of God nor regarded God's redemption plan. In other words, Abel took care of the sin problem in his life, Cain did not.

Genesis 4:6-7

"**6**   And YeHoVaH said unto Cain, Why art thou
wroth? and why is thy countenance fallen? **7** If thou
doest well, shalt thou not be accepted? and if thou
doest not well, sin lieth at the door. And unto thee
shall be his desire, and thou shalt rule over him."

God, in love and mercy, confronted Cain and invites
Cain to acknowledge his sin. Cain refuses, keeps his
sin, his anger and later slays his brother Abel. God as
he confronts Cain, sets up another courtroom scene,
giving Cain opportunity to explain his actions:

Genesis 4:9-10

"9 And YeHoVaH said unto Cain, Where is Abel thy
brother? And he said, I know not: Am I my brother's
keeper? **10** And he said, What hast thou done? the voice
of thy brother's blood crieth unto me from the ground. "

Cain's line of defence smirked his human
responsibility for care of his brother. Cain tended to
the ground to produce his first fruit offering; however,
his heart was far from God. Sin lay waiting at the door.
Warned by God to change, Cain refused to look at
breaching the distance between himself and God, nor
tend the problem of his heart causing the breach
between his brother and him.

After Cain's defence in this courtroom scene, God
passes judgment on him.

Genesis 4:11-12

> *"**11** And now art thou cursed from the earth, which hath opened her mouth to receive thy brother's blood from thy hand; **12** When thou tillest the ground, it shall not henceforth yield unto thee her strength; a fugitive and a vagabond shalt thou be in the earth."*

Blood, *the life of Abel,*[127] cried out to God from the ground. God responded to that cry and held court. After hearing Cain's defence, *which obviously lacked any form of remorse of repentance,* God pronounced judgment.

Widely paraphrased God said:

> "Cain, when you killed Abel, you killed the earth's response to yield its harvest to you. When you till the earth, it won't produce. You lost that connection, that dominion. You are cursed, Cain. From now on, you dwell under the rule of the baser elements of the earth that came in with death. You shall aimlessly wander about the earth, without a place to rest. "[128]

Cain responds with a request for mercy, showing he understood the weight of God's judgment.

---

[127] *Leviticus 17:11 Life is in the blood.*
[128] Wide paraphrase of *Genesis 4:12 but yet, keeps in line with its original meaning.*

Genesis 4:13-15

> *13 And Cain said unto YeHoVaH, My punishment [is] greater than I can bear. 14 Behold, thou hast driven me out this day from the face of the earth; and from thy face shall I be hid; and I shall be a fugitive and a vagabond in the earth; and it shall come to pass, [that] every one that findeth me shall slay me. 15 And YeHoVaH said unto him, Therefore whosoever slayeth Cain, vengeance shall be taken on him sevenfold. And YeHoVaH set a mark upon Cain, lest any finding him should kill him.*

Cain saw this judgment bringing 3 major things to pass in his life, the sum of which he could not bear. He saw himself:

- driven out from the face of the earth[129]
- hidden from the face of God
- as a fugitive and wanderer who, once found, would be killed.

Cain, who feared another would murder him, received mercy. God marked Cain so murder would not follow and overtake him.

THE WORLD OUT OF COURSE

After Cain sinned, God spoke about the consequences for Cain. Since the earth swallowed the blood of Abel,

---

[129] Not driven from a garden like his parents, but from the whole earth.

and it felt the impact of Cain's sin, the earth refused to yield its goods (harvest) to him.[130] An enmity existed now between the earth and Cain. This event and God's Word regarding the earth's response, presents an opportunity to realize sin's impact on the earth[131].

As humankind sins, those sins effect the earth. Just as Cain's sin affected the earth's response to his touch and would no longer produce for him, according to scripture, enormous practices of sins causes the earth to move out of course with God's divine order.

Asaph, a Psalmist, put it this way:

Psalm 82:5
   5   They know not, neither will they (people of wickedness)[132] understand; they walk on in darkness: all the foundations of the earth are out of course[133].

Here, Asaph speaks of a people's wickedness. Their wickedness, their great iniquities, kept them focused and walking in darkness. This behaviour caused the foundations of the earth to move out of alignment, to

---

[130] In fact, any murderer who followed received the same consequence .

[131] We often hear about sin's impact on a person's life, and while that happens, perhaps we should take the time and consider how sin affects the earth! This chapter provides that opportunity.

[132] Verse 2

[133] Online Bible from Strong's Concordance 04131 מוֹט mowt mote meaning to move, shake, be dislodged.

shake out of its place[134]. In other words, their sin impacted the earth in such a manner as to change its normal course of operation.

Putting this verse in context within the Psalm, Asaph reminds a government of its ills, who favours certain individuals and rejects others. He speaks of their need to reflect on God's desire to help the orphan and those living in an impoverished state. Governments, God calls into account, when they fail to defend the rights of the poor and needy. God expects governments to show no favouritism due to social or financial status.

Psalm 82:1-4

> *1 God standeth in the congregation of the mighty; he judgeth among the gods.2 How long will ye judge unjustly, and accept the persons of the wicked[135]? Selah. 3 Defend the poor and fatherless: do justice to the afflicted and needy. 4 Deliver the poor and needy: rid [them] out of the hand of the wicked.*

Failure to judge justly gives way to God's judgment due to the oppression it causes to some people of the land. Additionally, when those in authoritative positions elevate people into places of authority, who violate God's laws to further oppress others, it causes

---

[134] This principle, like all foundational principles remains in effect, today.

[135] Those who live apart from, or see themselves above, the laws of God, Who created all human beings equal.

142

further problems, which result in a negative effect in our environment. As quoted earlier in Psalm 82:5, the Psalmist makes it clear that such governmental rulers, those who oppose alignment with the laws of God's kingdom, do not understand, nor can they.

Psalm 82:5[136]
5   They know not, neither will they (people of wickedness)[137] understand; they walk on in darkness: all the foundations of the earth are out of course.

In their minds, their ways are best. Some alienate themselves from any thought of God, or His existence. They regard not accountability to God, but continue in their offences against God. As a result, the foundations of the earth shift out of course. When this happens the earth experiences violent storms, hurricanes, earthquakes and tremours, tsunamis, floods as well as draughts, which usually ends up causing famine. Unfortunately, Asaph never mentions that these men repent and realigned with God. Instead, Asaph concludes his Psalm by beseeching God for His government to intervene.

Psalm 82:8
8 Arise, O God, judge the earth: for thou shalt inherit all nations.

---

[136] This psalm, previous to verse 5, calls for righteous decrees in the earth by those who govern it. If that does not happen, the foundations move out of course.
[137] Verse 2.

REALIGNMENT WITH TRUTH

For humankind to live blessed by God, with the earth's foundations remaining on course within its created purpose, embracing God's ways become paramount. As Moses put it:

Deuteronomy 30:19-20
"19 I call heaven and earth to record this day against you, [that] I have set before you life and death, blessing and cursing: therefore choose life, that both thou and thy seed may live: 20 That thou mayest love YeHoVaH thy God, [and] that thou mayest obey his voice, and that thou mayest cleave unto him: for he [is] thy life, and the length of thy days: that thou mayest dwell in the land which YeHoVaH sware unto thy fathers, to Abraham, to Isaac, and to Jacob, to give them."

God gave the laws to Moses, at the same time knowing that our entire universe responds to the obedience or disobedience of them. To choose life, means to walk within the Laws God set in place on the earth. Such behaviour affects the earth in a positive way. Opposite behaviour causes negative effects.

Scripture teaches that humankind living inside the parameters of these laws causes the earth to remain on its course, thus preventing much hardship on earth. That applies in the life of individuals and, cumulatively in the lives of nations.

144

HEAVEN'S GOVERNMENT STEPS IN

Looking back to Adam and Eve, Heaven's government touched their individual lives at a very crucial point. After the first couple of humankind encountered God in the courtroom of that garden, they left that place to establish their own home government. As time went on, Cain and Seth grew, establishing their own home governments, too. Humankind continued to grow in number, and unfortunately, in great wickedness.

Genesis 6:5
"And YeHoVaH saw that the wickedness of man was great in the earth, and that every imagination of the thoughts of his heart was only evil continually."

With evil continually manifesting upon the earth, the purposes for humanity's life shifted into a downward spiral, with death everywhere.

Genesis 6:11
"The earth also was corrupt before God, and the earth was filled with violence."

To preserve an earth where integrity and justice ruled again, Heaven's government intervened. God enacted a judgment, sending a flood to destroy from the face of the earth the ones aligned with wickedness. He carried the only righteous ones on the earth through the flood, bringing them safely to the other side.

145

After the flood, Noah's family grew in number and
before long, civilization collected at a place called
Babel.   Disobeying God's command to scatter and
setting up a one world order contrary to the commands
of God[138], Heaven's government intervened, again. As
a result of that encounter and God's Word of
judgment, the people scattered.

Constantly, throughout Genesis, we find God's
righteous government behind the scenes and His hand
of judgment revealed. We find it:
  - in the call of Abraham as God called him out of
    a wicked place to be a remnant of righteousness
    unto God
  - in the call of Joseph as God sent him ahead to
    Egypt to prepare a place to save lives, both Jew
    and Gentile.[139]

As we move out of Genesis and into Exodus and
onward, we see God's specific call of the nation of
Israel. This nation God called to demonstrate His
Laws, statutes and commandments and live as a light
before all nations. This nation, once set up and
functioning as God designed, demonstrated Heaven's
government to the earth. Its model still does! We only
need eyes to see.

---

[138] Nimrod's activities gathered men together and formed Babel.
[139] God used Joseph to save Pharoah, the Egyptians of that era, as
well as the family of Jacob. Hence, God used Joseph to save both
Jew and Gentile.

OUR CHOICE

Heaven's government, that which functions behind the scenes, watches the life events in the life of every individual upon this earth. God knows the secrets of the heart of humankind, too. He warns, He watches, He rewards, and He also corrects. Our choice deciding how we wish to live must spring forth, now.

- Do we live for ourselves, allowing our human thinking, our wisdom, our philosophies to take us through life?
- Do we live for God, allowing His thinking, His wisdom, and His viewpoints to take us through life?

That choice rests with each believer, yet a true believer at salvation, whether conscious of it or not, already cried out to God, asking Him to bring His government to pass in their own life. Following that first commitment, comes the life of day-by-day choices to ensure we walk in alignment with the government of God in our daily life. Hence, Yeshua's words, Thy Kingdom Come. Thy will be done." (Matthew 6:10

NATIONAL CHOICE

Nations must choose the same as individuals for these, too, answer to God. If a nation builds their footings on the laws and commands of God and order their course likewise, they work in alignment with Heaven's government. Any nation who chooses to allow their moorings to rest upon human wisdom, using the imagination of their hearts to guide them, and subsequently, direct their laws and disciplines outside of God's realm of righteousness, and bring their nation out of alignment, experience the foundational shift of the earth, and eventually, come into a place of confrontation with the living God.

No matter how nations choose, whether for God or against Him, God watches, weighs out all matters, and then, rewards accordingly[140]. Truly, His Government, although unseen and often unacknowledged by humankind, *nevertheless rules in the kingdom of men!*

CHAPTER'S REFLECTION 👑

"Therefore whosoever heareth these sayings of mine, and doeth them, I will liken him unto a wise man, which built his house upon a rock: And the rain descended, and the floods came, and the winds blew, and beat upon that house; and it fell not: for it was founded upon a rock. And every one that heareth these sayings of mine, and doeth them not, shall be likened unto a foolish man, which built his house upon the sand: And the rain descended, and the floods came, and the winds blew, and beat upon that house; and it fell: and great was the fall of it." Matthew 7:24-27

---

[140] Give room here for God's search for intercessors to cry out for mercy. When His judgments finally come, they do so only after consideration of all the facts, weighed out on the scale of a just and righteous judge.

In the Creator's Call of Israel

10

"And YeHoVaH hath avouched thee this day to be his peculiar people, as he hath promised thee, and that thou shouldest keep all his commandments; And to make thee high above all nations which he hath made, in praise, and in name, and in honour; and that thou mayest be an holy people unto YeHoVaH thy God, as he hath spoken."

Deuteronomy 26:18-19

HUMANKIND cannot expect to simply fall into the knowledge of the Most High. While God puts a desire in each heart to know the Creator, only in seeking God do we find Him.

Jeremiah 29:13

"And ye shall seek me, and find me, when ye shall search for me with all your heart."

God desires all know Him, every Jew and every Gentile included. YeHoVaH promises that all who seek Him, from any people group, find Him. Only one condition applies: *to seek Him with all that resides within them.*

To help in humankind's search for God, in ancient times, God set the scene for one nation to know Him. From that nation, as the people within lived according to God's instructions, they demonstrated God to other nations about them. That nation of choice God called Israel. God visited this nation, and with His mighty Hand formed her. If Israel in her existence as a people and as a nation, kept the Most High as their God and kept Him alone, as well as observed the behavioural code given to Israel, then she would properly present the creator to the world.

Isaiah 60:1-3
> *"1 Arise, shine; for thy light is come, and the glory of YeHoVaH is risen upon thee. 2 For, behold, the darkness shall cover the earth, and gross darkness the people: but YeHoVaH shall arise upon thee, and his glory shall be seen upon thee. 3 And the Gentiles shall come to thy light, and kings to the brightness of thy rising."*

God's plan for the entire world to know Him, therefore, lay in the hands of this one nation chosen specifically for that purpose[141].   As other nations examined Israel, as they read or experienced the behaviour of her kings, as they knew her justice and religious system, a clear picture of God's character should spring forth for them to see. In other words, if Israel demonstrated God properly, to look at Israel - *one perceives God* and the way of salvation.

Unfortunately, Israel's history reveals that she did not keep only YeHoVaH as her God.   Israel embraced other gods and in doing so, followed pagan practices in her justice and religious system. Doing this, which at times included sacrificing their children to Molech,[142] distorted the image of the Creator, Whose character and behavioural requirements excel far above any that claim to be god.

As Israel wandered away from His laws and precepts in daily life and in governmental practices, God called Israel to return to Him. When she refused, eventually, God scattered her to the four corners of the world.

---

[141] God's choice of that nation did not eliminate the pathway for other people to seek Him. God responded then and responds even now to any who truly desire to know Him and seek Him with all their heart.

[142] Molech, a pagan god, demanded child sacrifice. If a nation experienced drought, for example, to sacrifice a child to Molech promised rain. This abomination God hated. *Leviticus 18:21; Jeremiah 32:35*

Nevertheless, God preserved or kept a remnant[143] to represent Him, in every generation. That remnant demonstrated the light of God to the world and kept the scriptures as a reference for their present generation and those of the future. Nations throughout history, which installed Judean-Christian values in their constitution, prospered. With the principles of God's kingdom at its base, a nation stands and withstands a lot. In the words of Yeshua,

Matthew 7:24-28
> "24 Therefore whosoever heareth these *sayings of mine, and doeth them, I will liken him unto a wise man, which built his house upon a rock: 25 And the rain descended, and the floods came, and the winds blew, and beat upon that house; and it fell not: for it was founded upon a rock.*
>
> *26 And every one that heareth these sayings of mine, and doeth them not, shall be likened unto a foolish man, which built his house upon the sand: 27 And the rain descended, and the floods came, and the winds blew, and beat upon that house; and it fell: and great was the fall of it. 28 And it came to pass, when Jesus had ended these sayings, the people were astonished at his doctrine:"*

As long as nations cling to the rock, they withstand the storms. These show God's character to the world.

---

[143] God always has a remnant. *1 Kings 19:18.*

If they drift away from their moorings, they begin to crumble.[144]

ISRAEL & GOD DWELLING WITH THEM

After Israel exited Egypt, arrived at Mt. Sinai, and there entered a covenant with YeHoVaH, they prepared for God to dwell in their midst. Eventually they built the Tabernacle of Moses to God's specifications. When it was finished and dedicated to God, a glory cloud descended over the place where they placed an earthly copy of His throne[145]. That showed all Israel that God dwelt amongst them.

As Israel camped in the desert following YeHoVaH's orders, they camped around the Tabernacle. Their camp presented a prophetic picture of the place of Heaven's government in any life, or any nation: *fully central*. That means all eyes, in all circumstances and situations, look to the King in their midst: YeHoVaH. It also means that all decisions, judgments, or problems of any kind, find their resolve in YeHoVaH, His laws, His commandments, and His statutes.

---

[144] Look around at the world today. Study those who began as Judeo-Christian nations, look at their present constitutions and see those which still stand and those which show signs of crumbling.

[145] Israel's copy of the throne of YeHoVaH in heaven we call the Ark of the Covenant. To learn more about that as well as how the Tabernacle speaks of Heaven, consider the book "It's All About Heaven", written by Jeanne Metcalf. ISBN # Textbook: 978-1-926489-32-2; ISBN # Workbook: 978-1-926489-31-5.

LIVING IN COVENANT WITH GOD

Whenever the glory cloud lifted, Israel moved to a new location. Levites (priests) carried the Ark of the Covenant, which represented the throne of God.

> *Numbers 10:35*
> *"10 And it came to pass, when the ark set forward, that Moses said, Rise up, YeHoVaH, and let thine enemies be scattered; and let them that hate thee flee before thee."*

As Israel moved ahead, she recognized that YeHoVaH fought her battles. He ruled and governed in their midst, and thus He decided the place where they must live, outlining the territories they must conquer for Him. As He led them, they followed.

HEAVEN'S GOVERNMENT WITHIN NATIONS

This picture of Israel camping in the wilderness with God's glory cloud in their midst, expresses an example of God's ability to move in and out of people's lives, cities, and even nations who embrace Him, His precepts, and laws.

However, even those nations which do not acknowledge Him, can still feel His Sovereign hand in their midst. For example, in Babylon around 539 BC, a king named Belshazzar, learned that God judged him and his nation. God's judgment brought that king's rulership to an end and gave his kingdom to another.

154

Daniel 5:25-28

> *"25 And this [is] the writing that was written, MENE, MENE, TEKEL, UPHARSIN. 26 This [is] the interpretation of the thing: MENE; God hath numbered thy kingdom, and finished it. 27 TEKEL; Thou art weighed in the balances, and art found wanting. 28 PERES; Thy kingdom is divided, and given to the Medes and Persians."*

This King, only a short time before, mocked the King of Heaven. He made tributes to Babylonian gods using the sacred vessels dedicated to YeHoVaH, which an earlier king brought to Babylon.[146] Belshazzar's lifestyle, arrogance, reign, and deliberate mocking of YeHoVaH earned him a call into God's courtroom.

Belshazzar's life required action. *"You are weighed in the balances"*, presents a courtroom activity showing that, on God's balance scale of justice, the king's actions and motives showed lacking when offset with God's requirement for that earthly kingship. God, after weighing all the factors involved, rendered a courtroom verdict. God found Belshazzar falling short of the requirements[147]. YeHoVaH, as Judge of all the

---

[146] King Nebuchadnezzar

[147] *"Daniel 5:27* TEKEL; Thou art weighed in the balances, and art found wanting." (Wanting means lacking or deficient.) In other words, Belshazzar's record of behaviour as a king did not provide enough evidence or good enough reasons to keep him on the throne.

Earth, numbered, finished, and divided Belshazzar's kingdom giving it to others, namely the Medes and Persians.

This courtroom scene over Belshazzar's life, human eyes neither heard nor seen. Nevertheless, God's Supreme Court convened and ruled. Out of mercy, the handwriting on the wall presented the decision, giving room for repentance. None came.

This scenario of God's judgment applies to all nations and kingdoms, whether people and rulers acknowledge Him as such, *or not.*

Psalm 22:28
   For the kingdom [is] YeHoVaH's: and he [is] the ruler[148] among the nations.

GOOD FOUNDATIONAL GOVERNMENT

In Israel's formation, in her years prior to her designated position within the Promised Land, whenever Israel walked righteously with her God, YeHoVaH, fulfilling her covenant[149] call with Him, she prospered. Whenever she stepped outside of that call by serving other gods, doing things her own way, she deteriorated. Within, she crumbled in moral decay, and without, she collapsed due to attacks from other

---

[148] KJV says "governor", however it means ruler, king, etc.
[149] That covenant call included keeping the laws and commands given to her: e.g. 10 Laws of Moses.

156

nations.

Israel's history with YeHoVaH speaks loudly. If she, (or for that matter, any people group), lives in a covenant agreement with YeHoVaH retaining Him as their God,[150] as they travel through the highway of life keeping their end of the covenant agreement, they prosper. God blesses them in their homes, their weather environment, in their land, in their economy, and every other place His scriptures describe. [151]

Conversely, if Israel, (or any other people group), walk away from their covenant responsibilities with Him, they experience oppression from within and without. Negating a covenant relationship with YeHoVaH means various problems arise as His corrective hand tries to realign His covenant partner.

Deuteronomy 28:45-48
> *"45 Moreover all these curses shall come upon thee, and shall pursue thee, and overtake thee, till thou be destroyed; because thou hearkenedst not unto the voice of YeHoVaH thy God, to keep his commandments and his statutes which he commanded thee: 46 And they shall be upon thee for a sign and for a wonder, and upon thy seed for ever. 47 Because thou servedst not YeHoVaH thy God*

---

[150] Covenant here, means a legal binding agreement with God whereby her leaders and people promise to obey His Laws, commands and keep Him only as their God.
[151] To see more blessings read *Deuteronomy 28:1-13*

In the Creator's Call of Israel

with joyfulness, and with gladness of heart, for the abundance of all [things]; 48 Therefore shalt thou serve thine enemies which YeHoVaH shall send against thee, in hunger, and in thirst, and in nakedness, and in want of all [things]: and he shall put a yoke of iron upon thy neck, until he have destroyed thee."

To make a covenant with the living God means solidarity with Him. To declare an allegiance with Him and then decide to replace that allegiance with others causes problems.

Taking it one step further, by adding or taking away laws to deliberately nullify the laws of God, to which others agreed, earlier, invites the just hand of God. As YeHoVaH desires to see them return to Him, the results of their choices move His hand to correct them. That correction often manifests in God overruling decisions made by humankind.

HEAVEN'S GOVERNMENT OVERRIDES

Whether a nation deliberately embraces the God of the Bible, YeHoVaH, or rejects Him, YeHoVaH still reigns. No scripture relates that God gave up His governorship of the earth. In fact, it states the opposite:

Psalm 103:19

> *"19 YeHoVaH hath prepared his throne in the heavens; and his kingdom ruleth over all."*

Psalm 66:7

> *"7 He ruleth by his power for ever; his eyes behold the nations: let not the rebellious exalt themselves. Selah."*

Psalm 59:13

> *"13 Consume them in wrath, consume them, that they may not be: and let them know that God ruleth in Jacob (Israel) unto the ends of the earth. Selah."*

Heaven's government, whether requested to rule or not, *still rules*. YeHoVaH, the creator, manifests His governing decisions *in accordance with His just and fair rule*. Humankind, created creatures of the Living God, best learn to seek Him early, and once we find Him, cling to Him all the days of our lives, teaching our children and children's children to do the same!

CHAPTER'S REFLECTION 👑

"For YeHoVaH's portion is his people; Jacob is the lot of his inheritance. He found him in a desert land, and in the waste howling wilderness; he led him about, he instructed him, he kept him as the apple of his eye. As an eagle stirreth up her nest, fluttereth over her young, spreadeth abroad her wings, taketh them, beareth them on her wings: So YeHoVaH alone did lead him, and there was no strange god with him. **He made him ride on the high places of the earth,** *that he might eat the increase of the fields; and he made him to suck honey out of the rock, and oil out of the flinty rock;*

Deuteronomy 32:9-13

(COURSE 202 CONTINUES)

Heaven's Greater Government

SECTION 3:
RULING IN THE
HEAVENLIES

(*After* Day 176s Victory)

In The Creator's New Creation

11

"Therefore if any man [be] in Christ, [he is] a new creature: old things are passed away; behold, all things are become new."

2 Corinthians 5:17

SIN, as shown in a previous chapter, affects our world, causing the foundations to move out of course. As it changes, things manifest causing things such as droughts, famine, earth tremours, earthquakes, etc. On the other hand, righteous behaviour such as repentance, which includes atonement for sin and turning away from wicked ways, realigns things with their Divine order. This brings healing to a broken land.

2 Chronicles 7:14

> *"14 If my people, which are called by my name, shall humble themselves, and pray, and seek my face, and turn from their wicked ways; then will I hear from heaven, and will forgive their sin, and will heal their land."*

Sin's payment through the blood of Yeshua on that cross, set things right, affecting our universe in heaven and on the earth. Clues to the impact His precious blood made call to our attention as Yeshua's blood entered the earth's crust[152].

Matthew 27:50-54

> *"50 Jesus, when he had cried again with a loud voice, yielded up the ghost. 51 And, behold, the veil of the temple was rent in twain from the top to the bottom; and the earth did quake, and the rocks rent; 52 And the graves were opened; and many bodies of the saints which slept arose, 53 And came out of the graves after his resurrection, and went into the holy city, and appeared unto many. 54 Now when the centurion, and they that were with him, watching Jesus, saw the earthquake, and those things that were done, they feared*

---

[152]John 19:33-35 "33 But when they came to Jesus, and saw that he was dead already, they brake not his legs: 34 But one of the soldiers with a spear pierced his side, and forthwith came there out blood and water. 35 And he that saw [it] bare record, and his record is true: and he knoweth that he saith true, that ye might believe."

greatly, saying, Truly this was the Son of God."

EFFECTS ON EARTH

As Yeshua died, the earth quaked. Some unusual things took place. That earthquake, like other earthquakes before it, opened the ground, however, unlike other earthquakes where the earth swallowed some victims,[153] in this earthquake, as the earth opened, the dead within it received new life! Resurrection power surged through certain dead bodies in their graves, causing them to wake up and rise up, triumphing over death. These resurrected saints entered Jerusalem (the holy city) and spoke with many people. Their resurrection, not hidden but exposed to many, spoke loudly about a mighty change Yeshua's death brought to the earth.

A NEW SHIFT TOOK PLACE

As this earthquake shook the earth to its core, Yeshua's sinless blood now in the earth[154], cried out better things than that of Abel[155]. When receiving Abel's blood, the earth demanded justice. After Cain shed that innocent blood, he lived beneath a curse, as the earth refused to

---

[153] *Numbers 16:32 And the earth opened her mouth, and swallowed them up, and their houses, and all the men that [appertained] unto Korah, and all [their] goods.*

[154] Many believe the Ark of the Covenant rested beneath the surface, and with the earthquake, it made a clear path for the blood to touch the mercy seat.

[155] *Hebrews 12:24 And to Jesus the mediator of the new covenant, and to the blood of sprinkling, that speaketh better things than [that of] Abel.*

yield its bounty to him. As Yeshua's blood entered the earth, it demanded forgiveness for sin and, due to the paid penalty of sin, broke death's hold, which resulted from Adam's sin.

As God raised the dead in that earthquake, He showed the power of death as broken! In its place, life ebbed, infusing resurrection power into some saints[156] of old resting their graves holding. Additionally, Yeshua's full payment of sin's penalty, made room for all humankind to live, forever!

1 Corinthians 15:55
> *"O death, where is thy sting? O grave, where is thy victory?"* [157],

Earth's foundations, affected greatly by sin, met with "life".

This encounter shifted death out of its master role, releasing its keys to Yeshua on behalf of all humankind.

---

[156] This resurrection touched those former ones who lived for God. While scripture gives us no clue to their number or identity, probably Abraham, Samuel, David and other saints who believed God received their resurrection at that time.

[157] *Hosea 13:14 "I will ransom them from the power of the grave; I will redeem them from death: O death I will be thy plagues; O grave, I will be thy destruction: repentance shall be hid from mine eyes."*

Revelation 1:18
> "*I am* he that liveth, and was dead; and, behold, I
> am alive for evermore, Amen; and have the keys of
> hell and of death."

Yeshua's victory has the power to shift God's crown of
creation away from death's moorings. All who accept
Yeshua as Saviour, seeing Him as payment for their
sins, receive an opportunity to live their life out upon
this earth in Yeshua's victory. That victory makes
room for the Spirit of God to ignite life within the
believer's spirit, helping them to triumph over sin.

All in Messiah, now capable of functioning in Yeshua's
power, walk the earth with the potential to live
victoriously for God. After the victory of Yeshua, as
the 7th day continued, death still effected humankind,
and it will continue to do so until God calls for the end
of the 7th day.

Then, as YeHoVaH brings forth the 8th day, death no
longer effects humankind. In the meantime, Day 7
continues, however, with a powerful governmental
stamp in place: *Redeemed by His Blood.*

EFFECTS IN THE HEAVENS

After the cross, as Yeshua entered the Heavens, things changed, therein. Part of that change touched the spiritual role of humankind upon the earth as God seated both Yeshua and those who live in Him in heavenly places. When He did this, His actions caused a new creation to walk the earth, such as the earth never saw before.

2 Corinthians 5:17
> *"Therefore if any man [be] in Christ, [he is] a new creature: old things are passed away; behold, all things are become new."*

This new creature, (*a believer baptized by the Holy Spirit into Yeshua*), never existed *prior to the resurrection.* Earlier humankind lived as the first Adam, a servant waiting for the Messiah and the promised victory over death. Believers in Messiah, *new creations*[158], receive from the life-giving spirit, Yeshua. Resurrection power surges within them. This infusion breaks the power of cancelled sin and places believers in a high place with God.

---

[158] *2 Corinthians 5:17 Therefore if any man [be] in Christ, [he is] a new creature: old things are passed away; behold, all things are become new.*

Ephesians 1:3

> *Blessed [be] the God and Father of our Lord Jesus Christ, who hath blessed us with all spiritual blessings in heavenly [places] in Christ:*

Believers, baptized by the Holy Spirit into Yeshua's death, burial, and resurrection, enjoy an additional blessing: *sitting in Him in heavenly places, positioned in Him for total triumph.*

Ephesians 1:19-23

> *"19 And what [is] the exceeding greatness of his power to us-ward who believe, according to the working of his mighty power, 20 Which he wrought in Christ, when he raised him from the dead, and set [him] at his own right hand in the heavenly [places], 21 Far above all principality, and power, and might, and dominion, and every name that is named, not only in this world, but also in that which is to come: 22 And hath put all [things] under his feet, and gave him [to be] the head over all [things] to the church, 23 Which is his body, the fulness of him that filleth all in all."*

This position, which came through the victory of the cross, elevates God's new creation above the normal, base elements of the earth. It positions them to function in a higher calling, more superior and far better than that of the first Adam.[159]

---

[159] That life, the new creation lives by faith.

POSITIONED TO RULE

Yeshua, in His discourse to His Apostles after the cross and prior to His ascension, spoke these words, which spoke of what the Father released to Him after His victory on earth.

Matthew 28:18-20
> *18 And Jesus came and spake unto them, saying, All power is given unto me in heaven and in earth. 19 Go ye therefore, and teach all nations, baptizing them in the name of the Father, and of the Son, and of the Holy Ghost: 20 Teaching them to observe all things whatsoever I have commanded you: and, lo, I am with you alway, [even] unto the end of the world. Amen.*

Yeshua, after completing the works of Redemption, received from YeHoVaH, His Father, all authority[160] in heaven and in earth. Sitting in Heavenly places, He rules, waiting for His enemies' total defeat, as they become His footstool[161].

All who truly enter the covenant of life with Yeshua sit with Him in heavenly places. In other words, Yeshua, sitting at God's right hand, holds the title deed of the earth. With that title deed firmly fixed in His Hand, He invites believers to join with Him in His

---

[160] Online Bible from Strong's Concordance, Greek word #1849 ἐξουσία exousia ex-oo-see'-ah. This word, literally translated means legal, judicial, deciding ability.
[161] *Hebrews 10:12-13*

170

governmental mantle, sitting in a place of governance with Him. This privilege granted to every true believer, constitutes a far better commission than the one given in the garden! With Yeshua's authority[162] accessible to believers, they watch, have dominion, subdue, and put every spiritual[163] enemy beneath Yeshua's feet. That privilege operates as believers call things into alignment with the will of God in Yeshua's name. Heaven's greater government, through Yeshua's death, burial, resurrection, and ascension reveals itself through believers as they live out their faith before the Father.

A POWER SHIFT

Death, the dividing force between humanity and their eternal life, met with a fatal blow. Death's *final claim* on humankind ended at the cross. A power shift took place, indeed, just as in the garden when man sinned. Only this time, the effect of sin's disobedience, God reversed as He received the ultimate payment for sin from the obedient and perfect Son of YeHoVaH. Believers in Messiah, in this new state positioned in the

---

[162] This authority which Yeshua possesses, belongs to Him alone to do with as He chooses. His authority, as stated in *Matthew 28:18*, there interpreted as power, means a legal, judicial, deciding ability. In other words, a governmental mantle to rule.

[163] A distinction must be drawn between the spiritual entities here, and those human beings who align with them. A believer's battle is not against flesh and blood (people), but rather against the principalities, powers, and rulers of darkness of this world, and spiritual wickedness in high places. *Ephesians 6:12*

heavenlies, learn to walk by faith above the elementary[164] principles of the earth.

Using the keys of binding and loosing[165], Yeshua's governmental term for acting in a governmental capacity, believers declare and see manifest God's power in circumstances and situations, all over the earth. With their faith in action, using the keys Yeshua put in their hands and His finished works of the cross, believers move in a new realm of power. This power, when properly used, sees doors open to all who wish to know truth and live eternally. In this manner, believers occupy until He comes again!

Surely, this position in Messiah makes possible a daily manifestation of God's kingdom wherever believers place their feet, and whenever their mouth declares, "Thy kingdom come. Thy will be done". Such a declaration reigns in this life in a greater way than ever before, due to the cross of Calvary!

LOOKING PAST THE POWER SHIFT

Most importantly, Yeshua's work on the cross effected the connection between God and man, changing things, forever. As new creations saved by grace, humankind affected by the fall, now enjoy the benefit of the redeemed works of Yeshua. All believers in

---

[164] Rudimentary properties of this earth, which God established, however, which He is not confined to.

[165] Spoken about in *Matthew 16:19* and in Chapter 7 of this book.

Yeshua, God positions in a new place with Him and in the earth. God's people no longer need to live as servants but by God's Hand, may now learn to reign with Yeshua.

Paul, the Apostle, put it this way:

Galatians 4:1-7

"1   Now I say, [That] the heir, as long as he is a child, differeth nothing from a servant, though he be lord of all; 2 But is under tutors and governors until the time appointed of the father. 3 Even so we, when we were children, were in bondage under the elements of the world:

4 But when the fulness of the time was come, God sent forth his Son, made of a woman, made under the law, 5 To redeem them that were under the law, that we might receive the adoption of sons. 6 And because ye are sons, God hath sent forth the Spirit of his Son into your hearts, crying, Abba, Father. 7 Wherefore thou art no more a servant, but a son; and if a son[166], then an heir of God through Christ."

Such sonship[167] exists for purposes of walking above the elements of the earth, moving with God in the

---

[166] Scripture refers to all in Messiah as "son". In passages such as this one in Galatians, "sonship" applies to any in Messiah, no matter their gender.

[167] Remember, not a gender term, but a term to show unity with Yeshua.

dignity He created for the crown of His creation, prior to death's reign.

Romans 5:14
"14 Nevertheless death reigned from Adam to Moses, even over them that had not sinned after the similitude of Adam's transgression, who is the figure of him that was to come.

That figure, as spoken about in the above verse points to Yeshua. Scripture calls Him the last Adam.

1 Corinthians 15:45
"And so it is written, The first man Adam was made a living soul; the last Adam was made a quickening (life-giving) spirit."

Through Yeshua, believers enter an unchangeable blood covenant with Almighty God. That covenant seals their redemption (payment of sins). Their covenant partner, YeHoVaH, promises to help them live within the framework of the new creation that He designed. Believers receive this gift from God and receive the help to live within the parameters of that new creation by faith. As they do, this impacts everything around them!

HEAVEN'S GOVERNMENT & BELIEVERS
Heaven's greater government still functions behind the scenes, however, after the cross, God gave believers

the potential to see Heaven's government function in a greater way than before the cross. That potential, when operating as God designed, makes clear the path for others to enjoy salvation, seeing a peace established between God and man. Its manifestation brings blessings wherever believers go.

In this manner, as believers do kingdom business, they engage with Heaven's greater government as it moves and intervenes in individual lives and corporate bodies[168] on the earth. Believers need only to remember this engagement in Heaven's government, looking to their ambassadorship for that government.

2 Corinthians 5:20-21
> *20 Now then we are ambassadors for Christ, as though God did beseech [you] by us: we pray [you] in Christ's stead, be ye reconciled to God. 21 For he hath made him [to be] sin for us, who knew no sin; that we might be made the righteousness of God in him.*

---

[168] Corporate bodies include cities, provinces, nations, etc.

CHAPTER'S REFLECTION

"But this man, after he had offered one sacrifice for sins for ever, sat down on the right hand of God; From henceforth expecting till his enemies be made his footstool. For by one offering he hath perfected for ever them that are sanctified. [Whereof] the Holy Ghost also is a witness to us: for after that he had said before, This [is] the covenant that I will make with them after those days, saith YeHoVaH, I will put my laws into their hearts, and in their minds will I write them; And their sins and iniquities will I remember no more."

Hebrews 10:12-17

Conclusion

"Verily, verily, I say unto you, The hour is coming, and now is, when the dead shall hear the voice of the Son of God: and they that hear shall live."

John 5:25

YESHUA'S victory opened an immense door of access to Heaven's greater government. Those who walk through that door discover many great attributes about the Creator, which otherwise they might overlook. For instance, Yeshua's triumph became part and parcel of a gift to all, for which God gave Yeshua honour.

Philippians 2:5-11
"5 Let this mind be in you, which was also in Christ

Jesus: 6 Who, being in the form of God, thought it not robbery to be equal with God: 7 But made himself of no reputation, and took upon him the form of a servant, and was made in the likeness of men: 8 And being found in fashion as a man, he humbled himself, and became obedient unto death, even the death of the cross. 9 Wherefore God also hath highly exalted him, and given him a name which is above every name: 10 That at the name of Jesus every knee should bow, of [things] in heaven, and [things] in earth, and [things] under the earth; 11 And [that] every tongue should confess that Jesus Christ [is] Lord, to the glory of God the Father."

Part of Yeshua's reward for His obedience to the Father and His victory on behalf of humanity, came as God seated Yeshua at His right hand, in Heavenly places. This victory Yeshua immediately bestows upon all those who receive His gift of salvation. By faith, they live positioned in Yeshua, risen to a place of honour in Him[169]. Likewise, this position in Yeshua for all believers, no matter the gender, reveals much about our God's character. Humankind need only to learn the language[170] of scripture to read it to fully

---

[169] These events, hidden behind the scenes of earth's event, powerfully effect it as believers learn to function in their capacity as authorities on the earth in Yeshua's name.

[170] Language here refers to the idea scripture conveys, not the original dialect in which God gave it to man. Understanding that certainly helps, but scriptural principles also teach the listening student much!

178

understand that God created all humankind as equal and continues to uphold that equality!

GOD SEES ALL AS EQUAL

Heaven's government sees all as equal. God created humanity in His image, and even though sinned marred that image, God does not consider this a problem which He cannot resolve. His plan for redemption, open to all, extends opportunity to humankind[171] to surpass their fallen state and share in the dominion of the earth, as given to Adam. All created humans upon the earth can arise to that position in Messiah. However, the choice rests with them.

God is no respecter of persons.[172] Those who seek Him, He rewards. Some He gives places of great honour on earth, such as King David.

2 Samuel 22:31-40

*"**31** As for God, his way is perfect; the word of YeHoVaH is tried: he is a buckler to all them that trust in him. **32** For who is God, save YeHoVaH? and who is a rock, save our God? **33** God is my strength and power: and he maketh my way perfect. **34** He maketh my feet like hinds' feet: and setteth me upon my high places. **35***

---

[171] This extension of mercy goes out to every person living upon the earth regardless of race, colour, gender or social status. God gives equal opportunity to all.
[172] *Acts 10:34*

179

He teacheth my hands to war; so that a bow of steel is broken by mine arms. 36 Thou hast also given me the shield of thy salvation: and thy gentleness hath made me great. 37 Thou hast enlarged my steps under me; so that my feet did not slip. 38 I have pursued mine enemies, and destroyed them; and turned not again until I had consumed them. 39 And I have consumed them, and wounded them, that they could not arise: yea, they are fallen under my feet. 40 For thou hast girded me with strength to battle: them that rose up against me hast thou subdued under me."

David's relationship with God and what he penned about it, shows his understanding of God's plan for humankind's dominion over all the earth. In David's time and in that of many others, that dominion manifested in the government of earth, however, it also manifested in other lives in different ways, such as those of the prophets.

Since the cross, Heaven's greater government still manifests, however, it primarily operates behinds the scenes as each believer learns to function in their God-given mantle utilized through prayer. Although earth does not see believers as a type of ruler, nevertheless, behind the scenes those functioning within their God given role implement God's plans and purposes. Through their prayer life, heaven recognizes their authority and place of influence.

Believers, in God's eyes, operate as part of His government when they function as He commands. Believers need only to recognize their position of honour and use it to its fullest potential. However, in doing their duty, since God releases free will to all, believers must learn to embrace the will of heaven, engaging with its greater government and its purposes. Paul, the Apostle, put it this way:

Galatians 2:20
  "I am crucified with Christ: nevertheless I live; yet not I, but Christ liveth in me: and the life which I now live in the flesh I live by the faith of the Son of God, who loved me, and gave himself for me."

Paul understood that to engage best with heaven, he disengaged with the desires of his flesh. Instead of living for himself, to satisfy his personal needs, Paul lived for his Messiah. His example speaks loudly to all who wish to truly function within the sphere of Heaven's greater government.

As believers crucify their flesh, learning to live for God, they learn to walk by the power of the Holy Spirit. In doing so, they further engage in Heaven's government to see it manifest over all the earth. Since they learn to rule in the spiritual world in righteousness, they also help to keep the foundations of the earth following their divine order[173]. This they do by personal repentance, as well as corporate repentance on behalf of others[174].

BEHIND THE SCENES
Heaven's greater government, from the beginning and onward, operates *behind the scenes*. Its operation, invisible to the naked eye, nevertheless impacts the world in which we live. Throughout this book, many *behind the scenes events* came to the forefront for you to acknowledge:

- **Pre-Creation**, where behind the scenes YeHoVaH called forth wisdom and established the plan of Redemption.
- **At Creation**, when behind the scenes God removed chaos and formed the universe and its elemental principles. Some of those principles included more behind the scenes events such as the calling forth of light, which divided darkness, as well as God's Covenant with day and night.
- **Adam and Eve's fall,** behind the scenes of a different kind, an adversary lurked to deceive and destroy God's sinless creation.
- **In Egypt,** as God's government, behind the scenes, overruled Pharoah's government. Thus, the children of Israel left Egypt with a mighty

---

[173] Psalm 82:5 effect reversed as they rule righteously, and walk on in the light, they positively affect the foundations of the earth.
[174] Repentance through intercession, etc.

Hand, journeying to a God-ordained homeland.

- **Daniel's life,** where behind the scenes events surfaced because of God's ability to resolve mysteries and speak truth to a king named, Nebuchadnezzar.
- **Daniel's companions,** where behind the scenes events saw the saving of three Jewish lives from a fiery furnace.
- **Jonah's life**, where behind the scenes a large fish cooperated with God to see the life of the prophet, Jonah, spared. Additionally, an entire city escaped tragedy as they responded to the message of the prophet, Jonah.
- *And more besides!*

Behind the scenes events discussed in this book pointed to the love and care of the Holy One of Israel, God Almighty, Who neither slept nor looked away. With face fully forward to help His beloved children who called upon His name, He moved Heaven's greater government into position. That movement brought forth miracles to overrule situations, changing their outcome and giving His people life.

Additionally, in this book you saw some of God's greatest hidden works exposed, such as the victory obtained at the cross. There, Heaven's government sovereignly carried out heaven's plans and purposes, all to the glory, praise, and honour of the Almighty. Looking at events since the cross, you saw highlights of the Creator's new creation, namely the born again, spirit filled believer. With regards to this new creation in Christ, you saw the Father's inclusion of this seed of Yeshua in the plans of victory for this earth.

BRINGING GOD'S IMPACT TO LIFE
As believers, let us grasp the fact that Heaven's greater government touches earth with God's sovereign intervention through the petitions of those who walk with Him and as they utilize their appointed place of dominion[175]. Indeed, YeHoVaH extends His hand of help to those who live upon the earth, for His heart desires the best for His creation. Recognizing that God chose to bring behind the scenes events forward, we see that He shows Himself as both interested and involved in the affairs of this world, capable of bringing to pass His reality for a world in desperate need for it[176].

God's plans for humankind and for the entire universe where humans walk and thrive, culminate in one word: *life*. If God's heart of love, mercy, compassion and true justice, humankind could only grasp, surely, they would choose in favour of His promised life.

Deuteronomy 30:15-16
"15 See, I have set before thee this day life and good,

---

[175] Dear Reader, if you are in Messiah, this means you!
[176] Perhaps, if more people thought about Heaven's greater government in that capacity, their alignment with His plans and purposes might seem easier to embrace.

and death and evil; 16 In that I command thee this day to love YeHoVaH thy God, to walk in his ways, and to keep his commandments and his statutes and his judgments, that thou mayest live and multiply: and YeHoVaH thy God shall bless thee in the land whither thou goest to possess it."

In choosing life and good, rejecting death and evil, people's choices align them with Heaven's greater government. In loving YeHoVaH, and walking in His ways, keeping His commandments, statutes, and judgments[177], these believers go on to live blessed lives. These, through faith, discover the key to victory in this life.

YESHUA'S RETURN

One day, when Yeshua returns to earth, and as the sky opens, the universe receives its new divine order. Under Yeshua's rule Heaven's greater government arrives in a fuller capacity than now. Until that time, living within this fallen world with eyes raised to heaven, believers have opportunity to cry out, "Rule over us". Early church believers put the message to God this way: "Come Lord Yeshua"[178]. Once Yeshua

---

[177] In other words, we live within the wisdom, power and strength of the Almighty as given through the Holy Spirit, Who leads us into all truth. Thus, we embrace what God determined as good, which includes following the precepts of His laws, statutes, and judgments. We live a life submitted to God.

[178] *Revelation 22:20 "He which testifieth these things saith, Surely I come quickly. Amen. Even so, come, Lord Jesus."*

arrives, one thousand years of peace falls upon the earth, changing our universe's present dynamics.

Isaiah 11:6-10

> *"6 The wolf also shall dwell with the lamb, and the leopard shall lie down with the kid; and the calf and the young lion and the fatling together; and a little child shall lead them. 7 And the cow and the bear shall feed; their young ones shall lie down together: and the lion shall eat straw like the ox. 8 And the sucking child shall play on the hole of the asp, and the weaned child shall put his hand on the cockatrice' den. 9 They shall not hurt nor destroy in all my holy mountain: for the earth shall be full of the knowledge of YeHoVaH, as the waters cover the sea. 10 And in that day there shall be a root of Jesse, which shall stand for an ensign of the people; to it shall the Gentiles seek: and his rest shall be glorious."*

FOR THIS DAY AND HOUR

In the meantime, until Yeshua returns, life in our modern world awaits the impact of Heaven's greater government. Even though the total dynamics of this government and the kingdom behind it, we might not *fully* understand, Yeshua gave us a key to open a door to align our life on earth with heaven's power. He did that in His address to His Disciples, when He said, "Thy kingdom come. Thy will be done." These few words uttered in sincerity, are the key to open a door for Heaven's greater government to manifest upon the earth.

These words provide a short cut for all people unsure of what to pray in any situation. If we believe God reigns and His kingdom promises better, uttering those simple words works to align earth's events with heaven. It works in the middle of pandemics, hurricanes, storms of life, or even if the foundations of nations shake! No matter the problem, no matter the depth or extremity of that problem, these two sentences possess power-packed potential to put it all right. Say it often: **"Thy kingdom come. Thy will be done".**

These words, when stated in faith and determination to see God's hand manifest to move earth into alignment with heaven. These two sentences, seven words in English, generate power enough to settle difficult and grave situations. These few words bring enough impact to shift evil from its domain and enforce God's power in its place. It only takes a moment of time to give them voice. When done, God's power engages to see His kingdom come and His will done!

Dear Reader, as we close this book, determine by faith to acknowledge God's activity behind the scenes of earth's events. Learn to put your foot down in a spiritual sense to see the kingdom of heaven come and His will done in every situation upon this earth, *local or worldwide*. Stand in your given place of access before Heaven's throne.

Lock your spiritual eyes to perceive the effects of the most powerful government in the world and beyond and state your case before the Heavenly Father to see the impact, behind the scenes of this earth. Take Yeshua's advice. Declare, *Your kingdom come. Your will be done.* With these simple words call for His Kingdom, and for Him to rule over us! Then, rest in the impact about to be made by

Heaven's Greater Government.

CHAPTER'S REFLECTION ♛

"For thus saith the LORD of hosts; Yet once, it is a little while, and I will shake the heavens, and the earth, and the sea, and the dry land; And I will shake all nations, and the desire of all nations shall come: and I will fill this house with glory, saith the LORD of hosts."

Haggai 2:6-7

190

APPENDIX

יְהֹוָה

YeHoVaH[179]

A Name to Honour

If, today, someone asked you to tell them the name of your earthly father, without hesitation you would declare it. If, for some reason, you did not know the identity of your earthly father, you would say so. You might even give an explanation as to why that might be so. Thus said, if asked to relate the name of your heavenly Father, today, would you do so with ease, or would you draw a blank?

Most of Christendom, today, is totally ignorant as to the name of the Father, as well as the way to pronounce it. As the author of this book, I would like to join the ranks of those who wish to relate that name to the world. When we stand before the Father on the day, we give an account for our deeds in this body, it would be a good thing to know Him, His Name and how it is pronounced!

---

[179] *Based on information given by Michael Rood. Some from his work entitled, The Chronological Bible, and some from his YouTube videos. For more information see page 28 of the Chronological Bible.*

Did you know that the name of the Father appears at least 6,828 times in the Hebrew scriptures? Scribes recorded it with four specific Hebrew letters. They are as follows:

י	Pronounced yode, or yod
ה	Pronounced as hey
ו	Pronounced as vav
ה	Pronounced as hey

For centuries, whenever the Jews come across these 4 letters they simply say, Adonai, or Ha Shem (meaning the name). They refuse to pronounce the name for several reasons, some of which we will look at momentarily. For now, let us look at whether their tradition affected Christianity. That we can easily do by looking at our Bibles to see the 4-letter name of the Father either written or substituted.

A quick look reveals that our KVJ Bibles, as well as many other versions, the 4-letter name presented to readers is a 4-letter English word, "LORD"[180]. Whether intentional or not, Christendom has followed the ancient tradition of the Jews.

AN ANCIENT TRADITION

In early second century times[181] Rabbis hid the pronunciation of the holy name of God. They did this by omitting the vowel pointings, which are necessary

---

[180] *In some translations it is GOD.*
[181] *Some scholars believe it dated even further back.*

to make the name pronounceable. Hence, as they carefully wrote the scriptures, their omittance of the vowel pointings made the name unpronounceable. Historians believe there were two reasons why they did this:

1. According to Josephus, Rome, under the rule of Domitian, 81 to 96 CE, put to death anyone using the name of the Jewish or Christian God.
2. Many believe that the Rabbis borrowed a tradition from pagans, whereby the name of their god was considered too holy to mention, so they called him "Ba-al" meaning Lord. The Jews adopted this practice and most still practice it today, even some Messianic Jews!

TRADITION CONTINUES
Bible translators followed their tradition for many reasons which are not presently known. It is possible, they forgot the pronunciation of the name, but more than likely, those who knew it, hid it.[182]. Whatever the reason, following this tradition caused Christians to continue in this tradition.

Does that tradition offend the Heavenly Father?

If indeed its origin was Baal worship, then we can give a resounding Amen to the fact it offends God. In

---

[182] *According to some, the Jews secretly knew the name.*

addition, as we look at scripture, we see the Almighty was not pleased with this, for His Heart desires all to enjoy salvation, including the Gentiles. How can that happen if they do not know upon what name they should call? Scripture [183] clearly says in the end times, Gentiles will know His name and call upon it to receive salvation. Obviously, for that to happen, they must know the name of YeHoVaH (יְהֹוָה).

AN HISTORIC DISCOVERY
Today, some Hebrew scholars[184] have searched the world over for Hebrew manuscripts. In doing so, they found many Hebrew documents have the full name with vowels and therefore the pronunciation of the name. These scholars may different slightly in pronunciation, but nevertheless, they are making the name of YeHoVaH known today.

OUR SAVIOUR'S NAME HIDDEN IN HIS NAME
In looking at the Hebrew root of the name of the Father, pronounced *Yah-Ho **Vah'***, and looking at another scripture, we see something amazing about our Saviour. In speaking of the Prophet, the one the

---

[183].*Ezekiel 39:7 "So will I make my holy name known in the midst of my people Israel; and I will not [let them] pollute my holy name any more: and the heathen (Gentiles) shall know that I [am] the LORD, the Holy One in Israel.")*

[184] *Nehemiah Gordon, a Hebrew scholar, according to his testimony, found the name of the Father with all vowel pointings in the Aleppo Codex, and through his efforts and those of others discovered that name with vowels pointings in over 2000 manuscripts.*

Father would send and to whom all must listen and obey, YeHoVaH said that His name would be in the name of the Prophet.

Exodus 23:21 "Beware of him, and obey his voice, provoke him not; for he will not pardon your transgressions[185]: *for my name [is] in him.*"

Our Saviour's name, as given by the angel was "Yehoshua", which means Salvation.

That name, with its Hebrew letters reads as:

י	**Pronounced yode or yod**
ה	**Pronounced hey**
ו	**Pronounced vav**
שׁ	Pronounced shin
ע	Pronounced ayin

The name of the Father (יְהֹוָה) is in the name of the Son! The first three letters of YeHoVaH show it! (Yod, Heh, Vav). Is it so amazing that the name of our Father is in the true name of the One YeHoVaH sent to redeem us!

<u>HONOUR THE FATHER'S NAME</u>
Throughout this book, and all later books, as well as all accompanying audios and PowerPoints, it is the

---

[185] *Please keep in mind that Yeshua bore the punishment for your sins. Your sins were not pardoned, they were atoned!*

197

author's intention to widely use, proclaim and continually pronounce the name of the Father, as well as the name of Yeshua. Indeed, this breaks with tradition of many, however, thus far as we have shared the news of the Father's name and use Yeshua's birth name, reception has been excellent.

NAME CHALLENGE

Since, as of this reading, you are no longer ignorant of your heavenly Father's name, we invite you to join the unofficial network of proclaimers of the Father's name and shout it from the house tops. In doing so, you honour the Heavenly Father, our Saviour Yeshua, and the Holy Spirit.

Romans 10:12-15

"12 For there is no difference between the Jew and the Greek: for the same Lord over all is rich unto all that call upon him. 13 For whosoever shall call upon the name of the Lord shall be saved. 14 How then shall they call on him in whom they have not believed? and how shall they believe in him of whom they have not heard? and how shall they hear without a preacher? 15 And how shall they preach, except they be sent? as it is written, How beautiful are the feet of them that preach the gospel of peace, and bring glad tidings of good things!"

ABOUT THE KING JAMES VERSION

Scriptures quoted in this book *originate* from the KJV **public domain version** of the Bible, which means, no copyright exists on this version of the scripture. While some find this translation outdated, Jeanne, trained in the KJV still finds this version helpful, and uses it in all her books[186].

In using KJV, however, it is good to remember the following:

- Some words in the KJV have changed meaning over the centuries. To understand such words, look up the root word in its original language. In doing so, the meaning stands out. For example, KJV uses the word "conversation", however, in its original language it means moral character, or behaviour.
- When KJV spoke of humanity, they said, "man". When you read that word, or hear others speak about the scriptures using the term "man", know it refers to all humankind, not a specific gender.

Due to tradition, the name of the Father, YeHoVaH appears as LORD, or at times as Jehovah. However, in all Jeanne's manuscripts, YeHoVaH's name replaces the term LORD. To learn more read "A Name to Honour", located in the Appendix section.

---

[186] In later manuscripts, the author updated the more archaic words in the KJV such as wouldest or couldest.

199

SALVATION'S MESSAGE

Yeshua, when walking on earth, said this:

John 3:14-18

> *14 And as Moses lifted up the serpent in the wilderness, even so must the Son of man be lifted up: 15 That whosoever believes in him should not perish but have eternal life. 16 For God so loved the world, that he gave his only begotten Son, that whosoever believes in him should not perish, but have everlasting life. 17 For God sent not his Son into the world to condemn the world; but that the world through him might be saved. 18 He that believes on him is not condemned: but he that believes not is condemned already, because he hath not believed in the name of the only begotten Son of God.*

During the time of Moses, the children of Israel in the wilderness, rebelled against God, at which time poisonous serpents infiltrated the camp, killing many of the people. After seeking YeHoVaH for a solution to the problem, Moses followed God's instructions and made a bronze serpent fashioned and erected it on a pole in sight of the people. Whosoever wanted to live, must acknowledge their rebellion against YeHoVaH, and in doing so, look upon the erected pole and bronze serpent, to YeHoVaH, who gave them life in place of death, then they would live.

Yeshua said, just as Moses erected that bronze serpent in the wilderness, He would be lifted for all to see. This referred to the event, in the future, of Yeshua's crucifixion. During the time when the serpent hung on that pole, whosoever wanted to live and not die from the serpent's bite must acknowledge their rebellion, their sin against YeHoVaH.

Likewise, for those who wish to live eternally, they must look upon the cross of the crucified One, to Yeshua, who provided life for them. This was an act of love for all humankind, necessary because man is born from Adam, and thus is born with an inherent sin.

Secondly, man sins. The consequence of sin is death, and eternal death, wherein man will spend an eternity in darkness, away from YeHoVaH. Unfortunately, there is nothing humanly possible to reverse those consequences. Even if a person had made a genuine decision never to sin again, and for some reason they succeeded, all their good deeds and good living would not erase the penalty of eternal death.

There is only *one way* for Eternal Life to touch a person's life. That way, Yeshua explained to His listeners, comes *through the cross*.

Salvation comes by understanding these facts:

1. Yeshua, being the Son of God and the fulfilment of the scriptures, never sinned.

2. YeHoVaH, on behalf of every human being on the earth, chose to make Yeshua become as sin, in His Eyes, so that Yeshua might pay the penalty for sin, for all of humanity.

3. Yeshua paid that penalty. He died on the cross and was buried in a tomb.

4. Three days later, He rose again, appearing to His disciples, to show them the reality of His resurrection, to show them God vindicated Him and made Him both Lord and Messiah.

5. Yeshua could not stay in the tomb, because "death" comes to all who sin, but since Yeshua never sinned, therefore, death could not hold Him in the grave.

6. All those who come to Yeshua, to receive Him as their Saviour, receive liberty from sin and from its horrible consequence, eternal death.

7. They enter Lord's Kingdom and receive eternal life, as well as another gift: **The Righteousness of Messiah.** After salvation, when YeHoVaH looks upon a believer in Messiah, He sees Yeshua's perfect life and sees a redeemed believer, set aside for YeHoVaH. Since salvation has taken place in the believer, the Holy Spirit dwells within them.

8. All it takes to receive salvation from YeHoVaH is receiving His Messiah, fully repenting from sinning

against God. [187] YeHoVaH even gives the believer the faith to receive His gift of Salvation!

The Apostle Paul put it this way:

Ephesians 2:8

"For by grace are ye saved through faith; and that not of yourselves: it is the gift of God"

When you pray the following prayer, realize we present it here to get you started in your walk with YeHoVaH. Living out your salvation depends upon your commitment to follow through *from this point, onward.* From the moment of your commitment and onward, dear one, please seek YeHoVaH for His help in all things, including help to make your life align with truth, and in the end be a praise unto His name, forever!

SINNER'S PRAYER
& LIFETIME COMMITMENT

Heavenly, Father:

I acknowledge before You, Lord, that I am a sinner. I understand sin's punishment is a life without You, for all eternity. Thank You for sending Yeshua to the earth, as the Messiah. I understand now that He died in my place, to take my punishment for my sins. I believe You raised Yeshua from the dead,

---

[187] *And against man. When a person steals, etc. they sin against both God and man. PLEASE NOTE: all references to "man", either by scripture or the author, refers to all humankind, not a specific gender.*

and now that I've I accepted Him as my personal Saviour, my old life dies, and my new life begins.

I humbly ask You to forgive me of my sins, and as of this moment, I receive Yeshua as my Saviour. I open my heart to receive the works of the cross that You provided for me through Yeshua, and with Your help, I will walk away from my sin, turning my back upon my own will and ways. I will now live my life seeking to obey Your Word and Your will. Help me to live, from this point onward, in a manner pleasing to You.

One more thing:

Remember, this gospel message comes with power. When you hear it, the Kingdom of God draws near to you. When you repent of your sins and receive Salvation, the Kingdom of God moves within. You cannot see it, feel it, or tell it from an outward observance. It is accepted, received, and lived out by faith! Seek out other believers in Messiah and may God bless you richly as you live your life, now, completely for Him!

So now, be sure and tell someone!

Remember that a person believes with the heart unto righteousness and confesses with their mouth unto salvation, as spoken about in *Romans 10:10:*

10 For with the heart man believes unto righteousness; and with the mouth confession is made unto salvation

OTHER BOOKS BY THIS AUTHOR (as of 2022)

Jeanne, up to this date in time, writes Bible Studies prayer books and devotionals. Bible Studies come with a textbook and workbook. Devotionals come as a journal, giving room for you to write your personal comments. **Note: books below are a Bible Study unless marked other wise.**

An Arsenal of Powerful Prayers [188]
> Scriptural Prayers to Move Mountains (Prayer book)

Arising Incense
> A Believer's Priesthood Watching

Candidate for A Miracle
> Wisdom from the Miracles of Yeshua

Foundations of Revival
> Biblical Evidence for Revival

His Reflection
> What God longs to see in His People

Heaven's Greater Government
> Behind the Scenes of Earth's Events

In The Name of Yehovah We Set Up Our Banners
> Biblical use of banners

It's All About Heaven
> As Pictured in Scripture

Kingdom Keys for Kingdom Kids
> Walking in Kingdom Power

Molded for the Miraculous
> Why God made You

---

[188] *This is a book of written prayers of various topics to help believers live a stronger, active faith. No workbook.*

Releasing the Impossible
The Limitless Power of Intercession

Salvation Depicted in a Meal [189]
A Hebraic Christian Guide to Passover
This is a Haggadah.

The Jeremiah Generation
God's Response to Injustice

The Warrior Bride-
God's Kingdom Advancing through Spiritual Warfare

Thy Kingdom Come
Entering God's Rest in Prayer

Watching, Waiting & Warning
Obeying Yeshua's Command to Watch & Pray
Comes with 1 textbook, 1 workbook, 1 prayer book.

When Nations Rumble
A Study of the Book of Amos

Worship in Spirit and In Truth [190]
The Tabernacle of David - Past, Present & Future

A SERIES OF DEVOTIONALS

Presently, a series of devotionals, put together like mini-bible studies, awaits its release.

Additionally, it is planned that by Year End 2022, Amazon will carry all of Jeanne's writings. To keep updated check Amazon or Cëgullah Publishing.

---

[189] *Haggadah (Guide) for a Christian Passover. No Workbook.*
[190] *Good sister book to "In the Name of YeHoVaH we set up our banners".*

SCRIPTURE REFEENCES

ABOUT THE AUTHOR

Jeanne Metcalf presently serves in the capacity of an ordained minister, working as the Senior Pastor of a ministry, named *"Forward March!"* Ministries (FMM). FMM is a part of a global grassroots movement of the Holy Spirit to return Christianity to its New Testament roots. Its primary goals include teaching early church concepts, spreading the gospel, and discipling believers so that all can walk in New Testament power, equipped to turn the world upside down with the impact of the gospel.

Jeanne gained credibility as a gifted teacher, writer, and speaker through her activities with FMM. With her passion for souls, a God-given insight and love for the Word of God, Rev. Jeanne presents sound biblical teachings on both the Hebraic and Apostolic scriptures, with clarity and simplicity, in a refreshing straightforward format. Those who study the Bible with Jeanne, highly recommend her studies.

Transformed lives stand as witnesses as through Rev. Jeanne's leadership, believers stand equipped, steadfast in their faith, prepared to live it out triumphantly.

To contact Jeanne, go to
www.cegullahpublishing.ca

211

www.ingramcontent.com/pod-product-compliance
Lightning Source LLC
Chambersburg PA
CBHW071946110426
42744CB00030B/513